People weekly
YEARBOOK
THE YEAR IN REVIEW: 1997

PEOPLE YEARBOOK 1998
EDITOR: Eric Levin
SENIOR EDITOR: Richard Burgheim
ART DIRECTOR: Anthony Kosner
SENIOR WRITER: Jill Smolowe
PICTURE EDITORS: Lisa Bentivegna, Samantha Hoyt
CHIEF OF RESEARCH: Denise Lynch
PHOTO RESEARCH: Sandra Mateo
COPY EDITOR: Ricki Tarlow
OPERATIONS: Denise Doran

Special thanks to Alan Anuskiewicz, Will Becker, Robert Britton, Betsy Castillo, Donna Cheng, Steven Cook, Bland Crowder, Thomas Fields-Meyer, Brien Foy, David Geithner, Penny M. Hays, George Hill, Suzy Im, Rachael Littman, Michelle Lockhart, Donna Miano-Ferrara, Eric Mischel, James Oberman, Stephen Pabarue, Adrienne Sayer, John Silver, Celine Wojtala, Anna Yelenskaya, Liz Zale and the Edit Tech staff.

TIME INC. HOME ENTERTAINMENT
MANAGING DIRECTOR: David Gitow
DIRECTOR, CONTINUITIES AND SINGLE SALES: David Arfine
DIRECTOR, CONTINUITIES & RETENTION: Michael Barrett
DIRECTOR, NEW PRODUCTS: Alicia Longobardo
PRODUCT MANAGERS: Christopher Berzolla, Robert Fox, Stacy Hirschberg, Michael Holahan, Amy Jacobsson, Jennifer McLyman, Dan Melore
MANAGER, RETAIL AND NEW MARKETS: Thomas Mifsud
ASSOCIATE PRODUCT MANAGERS: Louisa Bartle, Alison Ehrmann, Carlos Jimenez, Nancy London, Dawn Perry, Daria Raehse
ASSISTANT PRODUCT MANAGERS: Meredith Shelley, Betty Su
EDITORIAL OPERATIONS DIRECTOR: John Calvano
FULFILLMENT DIRECTOR: Michelle Gudema
FINANCIAL DIRECTOR: Tricia Griffin
ASSOCIATE FINANCIAL MANAGER: Amy Maselli
MARKETING ASSISTANT: Sarah Holmes

CONSUMER MARKETING DIVISION
PRODUCTION DIRECTOR: John E. Tighe
BOOK PRODUCTION MANAGER: Jessica McGrath
ASSISTANT BOOK PRODUCTION MANAGER: Joseph Napolitano

Title Page: Red Skelton, 1950s (Archive Photos)
Back Cover: The Spice Girls (Stephen Ellison/Outline);
Harrison Ford relaxing on his ranch (Timothy White/Outline)

CONTENTS

So young and Hanson: The Oklahoma brothers were as sweet as their sound (page 68)

Creator of Cool: Designer Gianni Versace (with actress Courtney Love) was slain outside his opulent Miami Beach mansion (page 36)

Proving "Queen of People's Hearts" even more in death, Diana was honored by fans in spontaneous shrines, like this one in York, England.

GOODBYE, DIANA

The Final Tragedy

Just as the princess seemed to find happiness with a new love, her life was senselessly taken

The day dawned full of promise. Tanned and rested, Princess Diana had just completed a cozy private cruise along the Riviera with her new lover, Egyptian-born businessman and movie producer Dodi Al Fayed, aboard a $32-million yacht owned by his billionaire father, Mohamed. Boarding a private jet, the lovebirds flew to Paris, then spent the afternoon of August 30 relaxing in the $2,000-a-night Imperial Suite at the Ritz—another jewel in the Al Fayed family crown.

As evening settled over the Seine, Diana phoned confidant Richard Kay, a *Daily Mail* reporter, and spoke of plans to step back from her charity work, a passion second only to her sons since her 1996 divorce from Prince Charles, 48. For Britain's premier ambassador of goodwill and good causes, it had been a satisfying year. Her itinerary had included Angola, South Africa, Pakistan and, most recently, Bosnia. In June, at the suggestion of son William, she had auctioned off 79 gowns at Christie's in Manhattan, netting $3.26 million for AIDS and breast-cancer work—and shedding unwanted reminders of her royal past.

Now, Diana said, she planned to concentrate on her private life. In a word: Dodi. Nothing seemed to roil Her Royal ex-Highness since pairing up with the dashing 42-year-old in mid-July. Not the paparazzi, whose rude intrusions she'd once likened to rape. Not Charles's recent public stepping-out with longtime paramour Camilla Parker Bowles, 49, whom she had referred to as the "Rottweiler." Not even the press reports that suggested Diana, 36, might be more dalliance than destiny for the celeb-dating, international playboy.

Atop Di's casket, draped in the Royal Standard, rode flowers from Harry, Wills and Earl Spencer.

Three times in the last five weeks, Di and Dodi had vacationed together, sometimes bringing William and Harry along for the fun. In a becoming array of bathing suits, Diana had stretched beside Dodi on boats and beaches, and beamed for the cameras. She had even raced up to reporters in a speedboat and teased, "You are going to get a big surprise with the next thing I do." As a result, rumors of a pending engagement were flying. ➤

5

Whether true or not, as Kay listened to Diana, he became convinced that his friend "was as happy as I have ever known her." For the first time in years, "all was well with her world."

After that call, Diana and Dodi drove to the Champs-Elysées, planning to tour Dodi's apartment before their 8:45 p.m. dinner reservation at Chez Benoit. But an oppressive pack of photographers, who had been trailing them on motorbikes since their arrival in Paris, persuaded the couple to return instead to the Ritz. Shortly before 10 p.m., they walked into the hotel's luxurious L'Espadon restaurant. Undisturbed, they locked eyes and murmured quietly over dinner. Meanwhile, Henri Paul, 41, the Ritz's assistant head of security and an experienced chauffeur, who had finished his shift three hours earlier, was called back to

Diana and Dodi seemed to revel in each others' company aboard the Al Fayed yacht off the south of France in mid-July.

the hotel. Though Paul appeared steady, multiple blood tests would later show that his blood alcohol level was triple the French legal limit.

When Diana and Dodi learned at 11:15 that some 30 photographers were amassed outside the hotel, they retired briefly to the Imperial Suite. After they emerged, Dodi dispatched his regular chauffeur to decoy the paparazzi. Then, the couple followed Paul out a back exit and climbed into the rear seat of a black Mercedes S280, planning to return to Dodi's apartment. With Paul at the wheel and Dodi's Welsh bodyguard Trevor Rees-Jones riding shotgun, the car sped onto an expressway along the Seine, where paparazzi picked up their trail. Accelerating to an estimated 90 mph, Paul drove into the tunnel beside the Place de L'Alma, then suddenly ➤

THOSE WHO HAD SEEN DI AND DODI TOGETHER DURING THEIR BRIEF ROMANCE SENSED A KINSHIP OF SPIRIT

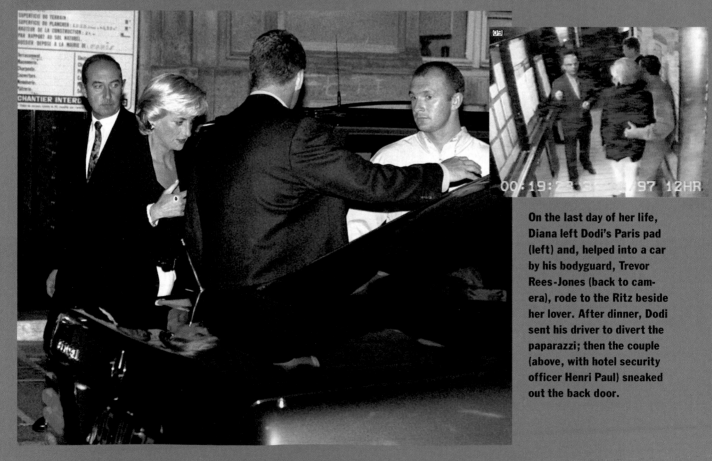

On the last day of her life, Diana left Dodi's Paris pad (left) and, helped into a car by his bodyguard, Trevor Rees-Jones (back to camera), rode to the Ritz beside her lover. After dinner, Dodi sent his driver to divert the paparazzi; then the couple (above, with hotel security officer Henri Paul) sneaked out the back door.

"Everyone needs to be valued," Diana (at a 1996 breast-cancer charity reception) once said.

Millions lined the streets for the funeral procession, many thousands having camped out through a wet, chilly night.

veered out of control (possibly the result of side-swiping a white Fiat Uno that police couldn't immediately locate). The Mercedes hurtled head-on into a concrete support column, rolled over and smashed into a wall before coming to a stop. Paul and Dodi would die at the scene.

Diana was found unconscious, trapped in the well between the front and rear seats. Emergency medical teams, worried about her rapid blood loss

SO MANY BOUQUETS WERE PLACED AT THE PALACES THAT CENTRAL LONDON REELED IN THE SWEET, SAD PERFUME

from internal injuries, spent 90 minutes trying to stabilize her condition before taking her to a hospital, where some 20 doctors and nurses struggled to save her. At 3:45 a.m., she was pronounced dead.

As word spread, grief paralyzed the globe. The Princess's astounding reach could be gauged six days later, when her funeral drew 2 billion people to their TV sets. The unprecedented tribute made it clear that Diana had earned the title she once said she coveted most: the Queen of People's Hearts.

Earl Spencer, William and Harry and Prince Charles bore up bravely as the cortege left Westminster Abbey.

Marveling at Diana's dawn-to-way-past-dark stamina, Renee Crown, organizer of her 1996 Chicago visit (here at a local hospital), said, "She was truly remarkable."

At Westminster Abbey, Diana's sons sobbed and friend Elton John fought back tears as he paid tribute to "England's Rose" with a version of "Candle in the Wind" tailored to the woeful occasion. The Hollywood contingent included Tom Hanks (left), Tom Cruise, Steven Spielberg and Nicole Kidman.

MANY WHO HAD RISEN EARLY TO WATCH HER WEDDING WERE AGAIN GLUED TO THE TV IN THE PRE-DAWN HOURS

The 75-mile journey from London to the Princess's burial site on the Spencer estate in Northamptonshire took 3½ hours.

"The best part of my day is getting home to the children," Diana often said of William and Harry (in 1990).

Moved by the extraordinary outpouring of grief that attended her daughter's death, Frances Shand Kydd, 61, decided to hold a memorial service of her own for Diana at Shand Kydd's local cathedral in Scotland. "She wanted to draw a line under the grieving and say, 'Let's get on with our lives,' " says Father Roddy Johnston, curate of St. Columba's in Oban, where the September 27 mass was held. Addressing more than 500 congregants, Shand Kydd reminisced about the "sunny days" of Di's childhood and spoke of rowing out to the Princess's island gravesite the day after the funeral for a private farewell.

Diana seemed to speak from the grave when author Andrew Morton released the transcripts of six secret 1991 interviews with her. Candidly she spoke of the "Camilla [Bowles] thing rearing its head the whole way through our engagment," her pre-wedding fears of being a "sacrificial lamb" and her struggles with bulimia, self-mutilation and a philandering husband who belittled her.

Diana's brother, Earl Spencer, 33, moved the world and stunned the Windsors when he vowed at her funeral to "continue the imaginative and loving way in which you were steering [the Princes] so that their souls are not simply immersed by duty and tradition, but can sing openly as you planned." But Spencer (below, with his latest lady, fashion editor Josie Barain) proved no better role model, settling an ugly divorce, in which he was called a "serial adulterer," for $3.4 million.

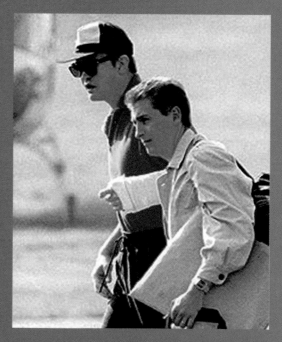

Perhaps because he was the only one wearing a seat belt, bodyguard Trevor Rees-Jones alone survived the August 31 crash. After he regained consciousness on September 16, Rees-Jones, 29 (leaving the hospital October 3), could recall early parts of the evening, but nothing of the fateful high-speed ride.

In October, Charles took Harry along on an official tour of South Africa, where they left their palm prints in cement at a rural Zulu school (right). While there they took in a Spice Girls concert (Charles bussing each of the five), and Harry carried out his first official foreign engagement: helping Charles open a Hilton Hotel. For reasons that are unclear, however, Harry flew home without seeing his outspoken uncle Earl Spencer. Older brother William, whose school break had come earlier in the month, remained at Eton. In November, Wills made his first public appearance since his mother's funeral, returning to Westminster Abbey to honor his grandparents, Queen Elizabeth and Prince Philip, on their 50th wedding anniversary. After accepting flowers from a fan, he got a teasing tickle from cousin Zara Phillips (below), daughter of Princess Anne and her first husband, Mark Phillips.

LATER, AS THE PLAYERS IN THE DRAMA SOLDIERED ON, 'THE BOYS' VENTURED OUT AND DID THEIR MOM PROUD

Her pageant regalia notwithstanding, says her uncle Jeff Ramsey, JonBenét (in 1996) was "normal, happy, healthy and bright."

'TWAS A YEAR OF TRAGIC MURDER (VERSACE, COSBY), SCANDAL (THE KENNEDYS, MARV ALBERT) AND MIRACLE (SOJOURNER, THE SEPTUPLETS)

HEADLINERS

Beauty and the Beastly

The killing of pageant princess JonBenét Ramsey continues to shock, perplex and shame a nation

From the moment JonBenét Ramsey's lifeless body was found in the basement of her parents' $1 million home in Boulder, Colorado, the mystery surrounding her Christmas 1996 murder has been a national preoccupation. Again and again, professional and lay sleuths everywhere sifted through the chilling clues: The sexual assault that preceded the brutal murder. The deadly blow that fractured the tiny skull. The duct tape that covered JonBenét's mouth, as well as the cord that left strangulation marks around her delicate neck. And, finally, the ransom note, a 2½-page handwritten missive that oddly demanded the precise sum of $118,000. Yet the same haunting question that ushered in 1997 attended it at the end: Who killed the 6-year-old beauty pageant princess?

The girl's parents, John and Patsy Ramsey, have been subjects of particularly intense scrutiny and speculation. To some, the millionaire CEO of the software distributor Access Graphics and his wife, the Miss West Virginia of 1977, seemed too good to be true, a hyperextension of the American Dream—even if they did sometimes dress their kindergartner like a French courtesan on her road to winning a half dozen beauty crowns. Is John, 53, actually an infanticidal monster? Is Patsy, 40, a driven perfectionist who—stressed by a grueling bout with ovarian cancer—snapped? And, if she did, was the precipitant the child's reported bedwetting, or the darker possibility that Patsy walked in on her husband molesting the child? Then again, perhaps the Ramseys *are* model parents, who after a dastardly tragedy must now suffer cruel persecution by the tabloids, the public and a Boulder police force that bun-

gled the early phase of the investigation.

To compound the confusion, the probe was burdened by strife between Boulder District Attorney Alex Hunter's office, which critics contend is shielding the Ramseys, and the police, who, in an unusual action, have retained three private attorneys to help build their case against the parents. Hunter, says D.A. spokeswoman Suzanne Laurion, continues to consider "the real possibility that the murder was committed by an intruder." That, certainly, is Ramsey canon. The parents, who raised eyebrows when they quickly hired lawyers and resisted cooperating with the police, have relocated to Atlanta, Georgia, where their son Burke, 10, is in the fifth grade. They continue to press their own search, which includes an army of investigators and a $100,000 reward for the killer's capture. Meanwhile, JonBenét's slayer remained at large.

The Ramseys didn't face the public after a May 1 press conference, when they asserted their innocence and offered a reward.

A Tragic Year for the Cosbys

Bill loses his only son and sues a self-styled daughter

The Cosby men caught a Knicks game at Madison Square Garden in 1994.

Bill and Camille left their New York City home after the crime.

The news was the sort that would have devastated any parent: A beloved son, stopped on a highway by a flat tire, is approached by a stranger and suddenly, inexplicably, gunned down with a bullet to the temple. The fact that the victim was Ennis Cosby, the 27-year-old son of America's favorite dad, only compounded the shock. Across the country, people found themselves murmuring the same words as Bill Cosby himself: "I can't believe it. I can't believe it. This could not have happened."

But it had, in January on a desolate stretch of road off L.A.'s 405 freeway, setting in motion the Cosby family's *annus horribilis*. As details of the slaying emerged, the horror only deepened. The gunpowder residue on his face, coupled with the pack of cigarettes clutched in his right hand, suggested that Ennis, a much-admired doctoral candidate at Columbia University's Teachers College, had been shot within 4 feet of his assailant while courteously offering the stranger a smoke. Indeed, Ennis's signature greeting to the many people in his life had been "Hello, Friend."

Two months after the killing, Los Angeles police arrested Mikail Markhasev, 18, a Ukrainian immigrant whose juvenile arrest and detention record showed a history of violent incidents involving African-Americans. Bill Cosby and his wife Camille issued a statement that they were "relieved and thankful to the police for their persistence," but the Cosbys' travails were hardly over. On the same day that Ennis was slain, Autumn Jackson, 22, a young woman who claims she is Cosby's illegitimate daughter, phoned the comedian's attorney, Jack Schmitt, with a threat: If the entertainer didn't pay her $40 million, she would tell the tabloid *Globe* that America's role-model father was a deadbeat dad. Within days, Jackson was indicted on charges of extortion.

Shawn Upshaw (left) claimed her daughter, Autumn Jackson, was also Cosby's.

Cosby subsequently admitted that he had slept with Jackson's mother, Shawn Upshaw, once (she claimed it was four times) in the 1970s and that over the years he had paid her some $100,000 in hush money. He had also set up a $25,000 trust provided that Autumn stayed in college, but Cosby insisted he wasn't the girl's father; he also refused to undergo the paternity test requested by her attorney. In July, after a jury rendered a guilty verdict against Jackson, he changed his mind and submitted to a DNA test to help establish Autumn's paternity. "He felt it was time to settle this once and for all," said lawyer Schmitt. But Jackson's attorney, concerned that the outcome might affect sentencing, declined to cooperate and have her tested.

For Cosby, the antidote to so much pain was to throw himself back into work on his CBS sitcom. "He knows this is a hurt that will never go away," said Dan Rather, who interviewed Cosby just weeks after Ennis's murder. "But insofar as humanly possible, he wants people to move back to the time where they saw him as someone who brings laughter into their lives." He also launched a Los Angeles-based charitable organization for work on dyslexia— which his grad-student son had heroically overcome. Its name: the Hello Friend/ Ennis William Cosby Foundation.

When she heard the original guilty verdict, Woodward cried out: "I didn't do anything. . . . I'm only 19."

Dark Victory

Boston au pair Louise Woodward beats a murder rap

Janet Burquest remembers vividly how she and her girl-friends felt in June 1996 as Louise Woodward, then a freshly minted high school graduate, prepared to depart their village of Elton, England (pop. 4,000), for a year as an au pair in America. "We kept saying how lucky and brave she was," Burquest recalls. "She was so lucky to be going to America for a year. So brave that she was going to be living with a family she hadn't met." If there was no telling what happy adventures might lie ahead, there was certainly no imagining the calamitous drama that would unfold.

On October 30, Woodward, 19, was found guilty by a jury in Cambridge, Massachussetts, of murdering 8-month-old Matthew Eappen, who had been rushed to a hospital on February 4 after Woodward called 911, crying, "Help! There's a baby! He's barely breathing!" For 11 days, the verdict stirred agitation on both sides of the Atlantic. Then came another shocker: Judge Hiller Zobel reduced the second-degree murder charge to involuntary manslaughter, and sentenced Woodward to the 279 days she had already served while awaiting trial.

Woodward, who had been facing a minimum of 15 years in prison, walked free that day. As she treated herself to a manicure, facial and shopping spree, her champions in America vowed to clear her name, while those in England celebrated raucously. "Has everyone flipped?"

"How can baby Matthew die?" Brendan (left) asked about his brother.

"She is a convicted felon," said Dr. Deborah Eappen bitterly (here with her husband in court), "and it has turned into the biggest opportunity of her life."

huffed a columnist for Britain's *Observer*. "A baby lies dead."

When Woodward set course from Elton, she hardly seemed a likely magnet for international celebrity and notoriety. She had lived her entire life in the working-class village, where her mother is a college administrator and her father is a carpenter. By all accounts, Woodward was enormously popular with her peers, who had nicknamed her Loopy Loo for her quirky sense of humor. Though a good student, she was uncertain about a career, and leaped at the chance to spend a year as an au pair. It seemed a perfect fit to the people of Elton, where Woodward had a reputation as a trustworthy and enchanting babysitter.

Woodward found her first assignment, 30 miles from Boston, too boring, and after five months switched to the Eappens in the suburb of Newton. At the trial, it emerged that Woodward had clashed with her second employers—Sunil, 31, an anesthesiologist, and his opthalmologist wife,

Deborah, 32—from the get-go. The Eappens complained that Woodward stayed out far too late on work nights, spending part of her evenings in Boston bars. By the end of January, they told Woodward to get in earlier or she would be fired. Other testimony suggested that Woodward resented the restrictions on her social life. It was her frustration, the prosecution argued, that

The Rigger pub back in Woodward's home north of London became an eery fixture of TV's global village, both (above) during the jury decision and (below) at the judge's reversal.

led Woodward to kill Matthew, five days after the Eappens' ultimatum, by violently shaking him and striking his head against something hard. Woodward countered that she had discovered a napping Matthew pale and nearly unconscious. She had tried mouth-to-mouth resuscitation, and, hoping to rouse him, had lightly shaken him. Minutes later, Matthew was rushed to Boston's famed Children's Hospital, where he slipped into an irreversible coma. Five days later, the Eappens took him off life support, and he died in his father's arms. Woodward's defense team maintained that the real cause of death was an earlier injury, perhaps caused by an accidental fall, that had inexplicably begun bleeding again.

The ordeal was hardly over. For the Eappens, both of whom returned to work, it would be a long time before their anger and pain ease. And Woodward, who had to stay in Massachussetts until any appeals are completed, found that freedom from prison did not guarantee freedom from judgment.

The Finisher of Diana's Fight

Jody Williams is awarded the Nobel Peace Prize for her crusade to ban landmines

When Jody Williams, the second of five kids, was growing up in Brattleboro, Vermont, she got so angry when neighbors teased her brother Stephen, who is deaf, that she took it upon herself to stick up for him. In so doing she found her calling: "Anybody who didn't know how to speak for themselves, I thought, 'I know how. I'll speak for you.'"

Those she has spoken for since 1991 include the estimated 26,000 people, primarily civilians, who are killed or maimed by landmines each year. As coordinator of the International Campaign to Ban Landmines, Williams, 47, raised the once-obscure issue to such prominence that she and her group were named co-winners of the Nobel Peace Prize. Perhaps more significant—and thanks in part to the dramatizing of the cause by Princess Diana— more than 120 nations signed a treaty aimed at out-lawing the weapons.

It is a heady achievement for the little-known antiwar activist. Williams was recruited six years ago by a Vietnam vets' group to run the campaign to halt the placement of hundreds of thousands of landmines worldwide each year and remove those already planted. Williams—daughter of a Vermont county judge and a mother who works with public housing projects—quickly fashioned a coalition of more than 1,000 groups. Still, President Clinton, citing a danger to U.S. troops in Korea, refused to sign the treaty but, pressured by her crusade, did announce a doubling of U.S. spending on mine-clearing. Williams had scolded Clinton for missing "an opportunity to be a world leader"—a role she plainly doesn't shrink from.

Knockin' on Heaven's Door

Dylan rebounds from illness to an audience with, and for, the Pope

He has his dad's brooding gaze down pat—but, oh, those baby blues. At 27, bandleader **JAKOB DYLAN** makes his own noise on the Wallflowers' triple-platinum *Bringing Down the Horses* CD.

His Holiness, Pope John Paul II, looked out over the upturned faces of 300,000 youths crowded into Bologna's fairgrounds. "The answer to your questions about life," he assured them at October's 23rd National Eucharistic Congress, "is blowing in the wind." It was an odd homage to Bob Dylan's classic lyric, given that the pop poet has said he finds spiritual guidance not in religious leaders but in the bleak, lovelorn songs of Hank Williams. Still, despite objections from Vatican critics, the Pope reportedly chose the aging rocker to perform—and listened intently, eyes closed, as Dylan sang "Knockin' on Heaven's Door" and "A Hard Rain's A-Gonna Fall." Then, removing his white Stetson, Dylan shook the ailing, 77-year-old Pontiff's hand, accepted a gift of a mother-of-pearl rosary and sang "Forever Young" as the Pope departed.

"I'm grateful to be asked," Dylan said of the show. And, he might have added, to be alive. Back in May the 56-year-old had been hospitalized for pericarditis, an inflammation of the lining around the heart—triggered, in his case, by histoplasmosis, a potentially fatal fungal infection. "I really thought I was going to be seeing Elvis soon," he said. By autumn, however, Dylan had issued a critically acclaimed and gold-selling new disc, *Time Out of Mind*, gone to Bologna and announced a triumphal year-end U.S. tour.

Gayla Zigo, the victimized wife, a military brat with ambitions to become an officer, got divorced and transferred from the scene of the scandal.

Conduct Unbecoming

Air Force pilot Kelly Flinn pays dearly for adultery

After a rocky first year of marriage, Airman Gayla Zigo felt that she and her husband, Marc, were making a fresh start in 1996 when they drove cross-country from Seattle to the flatlands of North Dakota. But on their 19th day at Minot Air Force Base, Gayla, 22, found a love letter to Marc written by Lt. Kelly Flinn, whom the couple had met shortly after their arrival. "I want to hug you so badly," Flinn wrote. "Just wrap my arms around your waist and squeeze." Attached was a key to Flinn's house.

Gayla's discovery would eventually lead the Air Force to threaten a court-martial as it charged Flinn, 26, its first female B-52 bomber pilot, with adultery, lying about the case and disobeying orders to stop seeing Marc, 24, the youth sports director at the facility. But Flinn refused to go quietly. Her family and her lawyer created widespread sympathy for the Atlanta-reared flier, portraying her as more sinned against than sinning. "Our daughter," said

Kelly Flinn was, as she said, the Air Force "showgirl" pre-Zigo, but had an uneasy private life. She was sexually molested by upperclassmen at the Academy and fraternized with enlisted men at the isolated Dakota base.

Marc Zigo, the cad in the case, cheated on his wife and ratted on his lover to Air Force investigators.

her mother, Mary, "was a victim—first of Marc Zigo, then of the Air Force." And Flinn, a crack pilot near the top of her Academy class, proved a persuasive self-advocate. Taking her case to a website and CBS's *60 Minutes*, she won support in Congress including from Sen. Trent Lott, who told the Pentagon to "get real."

In May, the service did back away from a controversial court-martial when Sheila Widnall, the first female Secretary of the Air Force, allowed Flinn to resign with a general discharge. But Widnall refused to grant an honorable discharge, noting "the importance of integrity to the Air Force and our absolute need to maintain order and discipline." Unimpressed, Flinn shot back by arguing in an article for *Newsweek:* "What matters in these cases is not what really happened but your gender, your rank and who you know." Her charge seemed justified two weeks later when Defense Secretary William Cohen tried to salvage the promotion of Air Force Gen. Joseph Ralston to chairman of the Joint Chiefs of Staff, despite an adulterous affair 13 years earlier with a civilian. Though the Pentagon's sudden lust to ferret out adulterers was looking like a witch-hunt, it was too late for Ralston. He will stay on as vice chairman, but, like Flinn, his wings were clipped.

The Army's Combat Zone

Charges of sexual misconduct freeze a hero's career

Retired Sgt. Maj. Brenda Hoster will never forget the afternoon in November 1996 when she read in the weekly *Army Times* that Sgt. Maj. Gene McKinney, 46, a decorated Vietnam vet and the nation's ranking enlisted soldier, had been appointed to a new panel investigating sexual harassment in the Army. (The service was reeling from its equivalent of the Navy's Tailhook disgrace, involving abusive drill sergeants.) "I just said, 'No way,'" recalls Hoster, who had abruptly retired from the Army three months earlier, inexplicably ending an impeccable 21-year career that had seen her rise to the top rungs of enlisted women. Now, she stepped up

to explain that on an official visit to Honolulu in 1996, McKinney, her married boss, had stopped by her hotel room and made a frightening sexual advance. Soon, five other servicewomen came forward, leading to McKinney's court-martial on 20 criminal charges, ranging from adultery to indecent assault. McKinney, who was suspended pending a January trial, indicated he would take no prisoners in his defense. While McKinney busily professed his innocence on talk shows, his lawyer presented a list of generals—white men—who had been allowed to quietly retire without prosecution in the face of similar charges.

Men Misbehaving Badly

Kennedy cousins kiss the girls, and make their wives cry

It was a banner year—of the tabloid variety—for the Kennedy men. First at bat in the scandal lineup was RFK's son Joseph, 44, a Massachusetts congressman expecting to run for governor of the state. Divorced in 1991 after 12 years of marriage to Sheila Rauch, with whom he has twin 16-year-old sons, Joseph successfully petitioned the Catholic Church in 1993 to grant him an annulment so he could remarry. Feeling bullied and demeaned by the action, which says that in the eyes of the Church her marriage never existed, Sheila finally vented her rage in a 1997 book, *Shattered Faith*—and then appealed the decision to the Vatican. The controversy stirred such clamor that in August Joseph felt compelled to bow out of the gubernatorial race but would stand again for Congress.

Adding to Joe's image problem

"There's a tremendous amount of love, even in their separation," said a friend of Michael Kennedy and Victoria (in 1993, with one of their three kids, Kyle, now 13).

"If I had agreed to an annulment, I felt I would be lying before God," said Sheila (at home and at her '79 wedding).

was his younger brother Michael, 39, his likely campaign manager and head of a nonprofit group that provides heating fuel to the poor. In April, the *Boston Globe* reported that Michael was caught in bed two years ago with the babysitter—then all of 17—by his wife Victoria (who is also Frank Gifford's daughter). Blaming his untoward behavior on a drinking problem, Michael went into treatment, friends told the *Globe*. But even during his stay in rehab, Kennedy apparently remained in contact with his teenage paramour, and the relationship resumed when he returned home. After the young woman admitted the relationship to her parents, she and her mother spoke to Victoria, who subsequently moved out. As with so many Kennedy scandals past, everyone involved seemed to wish the furor would just disappear. Neither the teen nor her parents appeared inclined to file a complaint—a necessary first step if prosecutors are to press statutory-rape charges.

Given all that, the flap that engulfed John Kennedy Jr., 36, seemed minuscule. In a personal mini-essay in the September issue of his magazine *George*, JFK's hunky son carved a distance from his scandal-scarred cousins by chastising them as "poster boys for bad behavior" who "chased an idealized alternative to their life." Jarringly accompanying the screed was a coyly seductive photo of a sinewy, apparently nude John-John posing as Adam.

Joe took the public lashing with a quip: "Ask not what you can do for your cousin, but what you can do for his magazine." He had a point. John had discovered a reader-pleasing formula that other editors have known for years: Write about the Kennedy men when they misbehave badly, and run shirtless shots of JFK Jr.

JFK Jr. stepped out with wife Carolyn , his hand healing from an unexplained but much speculated about injury.

The Wages of Sin

A jilted wife gets even—and a $1 million court award—by suing the rival for her affections

It started with a nasty rumor. Dorothy Hutelmyer was in the parking lot of a Burlington, North Carolina, elementary school in 1995 when a friend reported hearing that she was about to split with Joseph Hutelmyer—the college sweetheart with whom she had three sons, a handsome red brick house and, as far as she knew, a perfectly happy marriage of 17 years. "At the time, I laughed," says Hutelmyer, 40. But within a month, she was weeping. Joe, 43, a successful insurance executive, left her for another woman, his longtime administrative assistant Margie Cox, 39. "I decided this was wrong. This woman does not have the right to break up a strong, loving marriage," says Hutelmyer. "And I thought, 'What am I going to do about it?' "

She decided to get revenge. By dusting off a century-old North Carolina law designed to protect husbands and wives from predatory home wreckers, Hutelmyer filed a suit against Cox for "alienation of affection"—in plain English, for stealing her man by relentless flirting. In a

decision that instantly gave heart to jilted spouses everywhere, a jury sided with the spurned wife and ordered Cox to pay Hutelmyer $1 million. "She's a sinner," says Hutelmyer. "What she did was against the laws of society."

Cox, now the second Mrs. Hutelmyer, counters that she began an affair with her boss in 1994 only after he had assured her that his marriage was empty and beyond repair. Cox, at the time a recently divorced mother of two, explains that she "reacted the way a lot of people do who are newly divorced. I was doing what I could to feel better about myself." While she got the man, the previous Mrs. Hutelmyer got $4,000 in monthly child support, the promise of a seven-figure settlement and the final word on her cheating ex-husband. "I know this sounds crazy," she says, "but I think he's a good person who did something, well, something very stupid."

Dorothy Hutelmyer got love poems for 15 years from Joe (above, in 1995); now he's re-wed, she's a paralegal.

A Heroic Redressing of History

Swiss security guard Christoph Meili saves Nazi-era bank papers

A devout Protestant, Christoph Meili hardly seemed a likely candidate to force the Swiss to revisit its banking practices during the Nazi era. But on January 9, while making his rounds as a night watchman at the Union Bank of Switzerland headquarters in Zurich, Meili, 29, poked his head into the shredding room, where he spotted two carts filled with documents waiting to be destroyed. When Meili looked closer, he noticed that some of the bank papers concerned dealings with Germany during the 1940s, including the sale of confiscated properties. Aware that recent Swiss regulations prohibited the destruction of records that might shed light on the nation's wartime banking activities, Meili snatched two ledgers, plus pages from a third, then turned the cache over to Zurich's Hebrew Congregation. By the time the papers reached the police, Meili was already suspended from his security job, pending investigation into violation of bank-secrecy laws. Within two months, Meili was fired; within four, he fled Switzerland, fearing for his life because of death threats. If perceived as a snitch at home (where an investigation into his actions was eventually dropped), Meili was hailed as a hero abroad. Israel's Knesset offered Meili an expense-paid trip to the Holy Land, while U.S. tycoon Edgar Bronfman, president of the World Jewish Congress, offered him a job. Meili, his wife and two children are now permanent residents of the U.S.

Learning About The Fast Lane

Skater Oksana Baiul gets her act together after careening dangerously out of control

Whether it was the stress of meeting the high expectations that attend an Olympic gold medal, the excess or success or simply growing pains, Ukrainian figure skater Oksana Baiul, 19, had been doing more partying than practicing. Then, in the wee hours of January 12, she nearly lost everything. Returning from an ice pageant to her nine-room home in Simsbury, Connecticut, she stopped at a bar and downed several Long Island iced teas, a potent mix of vodka, gin, rum and tequila. Later at the wheel of her green Mercedes and traveling at what police estimate was close to 100 mph, she skidded off the two-lane highway and into some bushes. Baiul, who sustained a mild concussion and a scalp wound, believes she was protected by a guardian angel—her mother, who died of ovarian cancer in 1991. "After my accident," she says, "I put her cross around my neck, and I will never take it off."

Baiul took a required alcohol educa-

D.W.I. charges were dropped after she paid a $90 fine and took a rehab course.

tion program—and stock of her life. She stopped drinking, replaced her longtime coach, signed with a new show and parted ways with some old pals. "I want to build a new Oksana," she said, "and I'm getting there."

Skating on Thin Ice

Olympic champ Scott Hamilton wages a heroic battle with cancer

Ever since Scott Hamilton won the 1984 Olympic gold medal, Americans have felt a personal bond with the diminutive, upbeat figure skater. Maybe it was his scrappy triumph over a hard-luck start as the scrawny kid who spent much of his early childhood in and out of hospitals with the malabsorption syndrome that stunted his growth. Or maybe it was his engaging personality on ice and as a TV commentator. So fans and fellow skaters alike were worried when Hamilton, just 39, left the *Stars on Ice* tour last March to deal with a challenge far more treacherous than his signature back flip: testicular cancer. While 55,000 well-wishes poured in from around the country, Hamilton underwent four cycles of chemotherapy to shrink a tumor twice the size of a grapefruit. For him, the ordeal was particularly frightening; his mother had died of cancer when he was 18. But on October 29, Hamilton returned to the ice (right) to a standing ovation and a prognosis for full recovery.

The Clintons beamed
proudly after Chelsea's
graduation ceremony
at the Sidwell Friends
School.

A Chelsea Dawning

Flown from the nest, the First Daughter settles in at Stanford like any other freshman. Yeah, right

Posh campuses have seen their share of celebs before. Yale got Jodi Foster; Princeton got Brooke Shields. Even so, when Chelsea Clinton turned up in California to register as First Freshman at Stanford, her arrival was as clamorous as a homecoming rally: a two-block motorcade, a contingent of 200-odd journalists not to mention a Secret Service detail and a temporary gauntlet of metal detectors. There was something surreal even when her father brought out a toolbox to pound picture hooks in her dorm-room wall. Just call him the Carpenter-in-Chief.

But roughly four hours after the President and First Lady had cleared out, some semblance of normality returned—which is to say, a whole lot of goofy behavior. There was Chelsea, 17, with a couple of hundred other frosh shortly before midnight, trailing a school band from dorm to dorm, ending at the main quad with a

rousing rendition of Stanford University's fight song. Says Woojin Park, a sophomore: "She looked like she was having a great time."

Both Chelsea and her parents are hoping her college years will bring more of the same. Chelsea—whose Secret Service handle is reportedly Energy—will have her usual escort of bodyguards. But the young agents brought in for her detail will dress casually. And Chelsea's privacy is being safeguarded so rigorously that the White House refused to disclose her roommate's name. As the First Lady explained in one of her syndicated columns, growing up is tough enough without "the extra pressure of press and public scrutiny."

At a pre-prom party last spring (above), Chelsea got cozy—for the cameras, that is—with date Bobby Lutzker; in the fall, she turned out to support Stanford's football team.

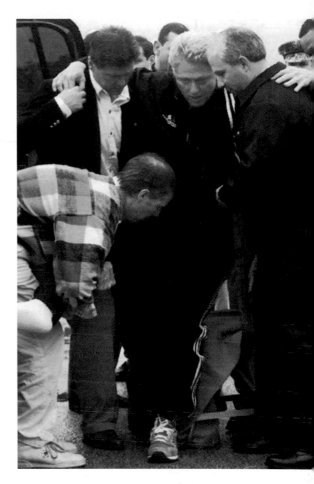

THE ULTIMATE POWER TRIP

It was the pop heard round the world. On March 14, President Clinton slipped on a dimly lit wooden step outside golfer Greg Norman's home in Hobe Sound, Florida, rupturing his right quadriceps tendon—the connective tissue that binds the muscles of the thigh to the kneecap. After an emergency-room check, he flew home to Bethesda Naval Hospital for surgery. Clinton, 50, was willing to accept only painkillers that would allow him to remain alert during the two-hour procedure. Five days later, he jetted off to Helsinki, determined not to be slowed by the injury. Two months later, three weeks ahead of schedule, he graduated from crutches to a cane. Throughout his ordeal, he paid close attention to how his body is aging. "The most important thing I've learned," he said, "is how to do the proper stretching exercises."

Silver Statement

What becomes a legend most? For Liz Taylor, a truth-in-packaging coiffure after brain surgery

---

Shortly after he removed a 2-inch tumor from Elizabeth Taylor's brain in February, Dr. Martin Cooper held up a few everyday objects to make sure his star patient could identify them. When he showed her a wedding band, Cooper recalls, the famous violet eyes flashed mischievously. " 'Oh,' " Cooper says Taylor joked, " 'I've had many of those!' "

The benign tumor had been discovered after Taylor experienced headaches and doctors ordered a brain scan February 3. Taylor refused, however, to focus on her own health until after the February 16 taping of her TV special, *Happy Birthday, Elizabeth: A Celebration of Life*—a 65th-birthday gala designed to benefit Taylor's impassioned cause, AIDS. Then she checked into Cedars-Sinai Medical Center in Los Angeles, where she received hundreds of cards from fans, flowers from celebrated friends such as Michael Jackson, and visits by the four grown children from her eight marriages.

The golfball-size tumor was the latest in a series of serious ailments Taylor has suffered. As with the pneumonia and hip replacements that came before, she proved feisty. "She faces this kind of situation better than anyone I've seen," said her lawyer Neil Papiano. "Maybe that's because she's had to face so much adversity." Taylor's scalp was shaved for the three-hour surgery, in which doctors inserted titanium microplates into her skull behind her left ear. As Taylor ended her eight-day hospital stay, she joked, "I don't mind being bald. For years the gossips have been claiming that I've been having face-lifts. Now they'll have to eat their words. No scars." Then the twice-Oscared Taylor went home to recuperate.

Six months later when Hollywood's favorite fundraiser made her public reappearance—in Istanbul, Turkey, at an event to benefit the children of war-ravaged Chechnya—she was startlingly silver. Gone were her trademark tresses, the haystack of raven locks. Taylor had ceased dyeing her hair and boldly cropped it short. Demonstrating she was still, as ever, a natural knockout.

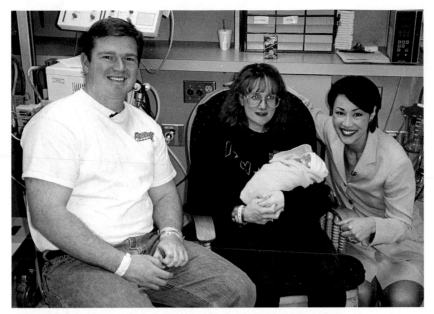

Bobbi (holding Kenneth, with hubby and *Dateline*'s Ann Curry) told the show, "When God gives you something . . . there's a purpose." At right: all seven, in birth order.

Iowa's Magnificent Seven

Bobbi and Kenny McCaughey gird for 350 diaper changes a week

Bobbi McCaughey understood that by taking the fertility drug Metrodin, she had a 15 percent greater chance of a multiple birth. But in her mind, that meant twins, possibly even triplets—or maybe just one, as had been the case with her first child, Mikayla, now 2, who had similarly been conceived with the aid of Metrodin. So Bobbi, 29, a former seamstress, was certainly not prepared for what an ultrasound showed last spring. "Seven?" gasped her husband, Kenny, 27, a billing clerk at a Chevrolet dealership in their hometown of Carlisle, Iowa. "What is the Lord doing here?"

Working wonders. Word of the pregnancy soon spread through town, but the people of Carlisle (pop. 3,240) hugged the McCaugheys' secret amazingly tight. Then, on November 19, the entire world found out when Bobbi, assisted by a 40-person medical team, gave birth by cesarean section to the first-ever thriving set of septuplets: four boys and three girls, ranging in size from 3 lbs. 4-oz. down to 2 lbs. 5 oz. Following the deliveries, doctors had to grapple with some worrisome developments. All the babies were initially put on ventilators, and the last-born required a blood transfusion. Still, according to the best scientific estimates, Bobbi had stood a greater chance of being struck dead by an asteroid than carrying the seven babies to term. The Thanksgiving-season miracle produced an unprecedented bounty of gift offers, including a lifetime supply of diapers (from the Pampers people), a new house (from local businesses) and free college educations (from St. Ambrose University in Davenport).

Through it all, Bobbi, the oldest of six children of a Baptist minister, clung calmly to her Christian faith. Never once during her pregnancy did she waver from her conviction that she would have all seven rather than opt for "fetal reduction," the medical term for selective abortion to enhance the remaining babies' chances of survival. And just four days after the delivery, she walked, unaided, across the threshold of her tiny three-bedroom home, secure in the knowledge that each of her babies seemed to have survived the trauma of birth whole and undamaged. "I know that it's extraordinary or whatever to have this many babies and go this far," she said. "I wanted them."

1. KENNETH ROBERT

2. ALEXIS MAY

3. NATALIE SUE

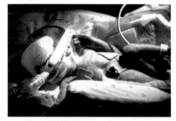

4. KELSEY ANN

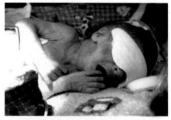

5. BRANDON JAMES

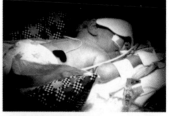

6. NATHAN ROY

7. JOEL STEVEN

With Weight Watchers'
Kathy Zajackowski (and
her "before" picture),
Fergie confided to the
press that she had once
ballooned to 200 lbs.

Royal Pitch

To trim her debt, Fergie trades pounds for dollars

When your taste for the high life has racked up a debt of $7.1 million and your divorce settlement is a measly $2.85 million, what's a woman to do? For Sarah Ferguson, 38, the disgraced Duchess of York, the solution was typically antipodal. Domestically, she moved back into Andrew's home, Sunninghill, to cut living costs, but, commercially, she fled overseas, far from the imperious glare of her ex-mother-in-law, to shill her way to solvency.

In Australia, Fergie earned a reported $75,000 for digging a cable trough to publicize a pay-TV network. In Austria, she attended an opera ball for $40,000 and appeared in print ads for Olympus cameras. And in France, *Paris Match* paid her $500,000 to debrief celebrities.

Ubiquitous in the U.S., Fergie shot a pair of TV spots for Ocean Spray Lightstyle juices, pretending, through 103-odd takes, to throw a bucket of ice on photographers. (Her fee: an estimated $845,000.) Next, the woman once known as the Duchess of Pork became the spokeswoman for Weight Watchers, a year-long, $1 million-plus gig. But nothing proved so profitable as the peddling of her royal self in an autobiography, grandly titled *My Story* and netting a tidy $3.7 million. She chatted up the book so effectively with the likes of Oprah, Letterman and Leno that she cleared her debt—except for her, ahem, $2.7 million tax bill. So, Fergie rounded out the year by filming an ABC-TV special about extraordinary people. That she is.

WHAT'S A BILLION BETWEEN FRIENDS?

"I'm putting every rich person in the world on notice," warned Ted Turner on CNN's *Larry King Live.* "They're going to be hearing from me." Whether it was a veiled threat or a friendly ribbing, the CNN founder and vice chairman of Time Warner (publisher of PEOPLE) had earned the right to call in the charity chips: Earlier that September evening, he had stunned the world by announcing at a United Nations Association dinner in his honor (above) that over the next decade he will contribute $1 billion to U.N. efforts. One of the largest single donations ever, it will be put in a foundation aimed at assisting children and refugees, clearing landmines and fighting disease. Turner, 58, seems to have been bitten by the philanthropy bug—or perhaps by wife Jane Fonda, a longtime paladin of public (if not not always politically popular) causes. A few months before, the Mouth of the South had scolded fellow billionaires Bill Gates and Warren Buffett for not being generous enough. "What good," asked Turner, "is wealth sitting in the bank?"

Turning 60 didn't cool Jane Fonda's crusading life. Her '97 fight: teen pregnancy.

Blood on the Steps

A serial killer guns down fashion titan Gianni Versace

pproaching the cheery green awnings of South Beach's trendy News Cafe on the morning of July 15, just as the last sweaty revelers were straggling home from the Miami clubs, Gianni Versace, 50, seemed to some observers uncharacteristically preoccupied. The Italian fashion designer, who had draped every part of the celebrity spectrum, from royalty to rappers, whose phototropic creations had melded rock swagger with runway hauteur, walked past the restaurant, then backtracked and stepped inside. But instead of sitting to savor his usual morning *café*, he grabbed a handful of magazines, paid and left. Versace may have sensed something was amiss, and indeed it was. Minutes later, as he was opening the ornate wrought-iron gates to Casa Casuarina, the Mediterranean-style palazzo where Versace routinely entertained pals such as Madonna and Sly Stallone, he was approached by a young man wearing a white shirt, gray shorts and a black backpack. The two were reportedly seen struggling over a bag Versace was holding, then two shots rang out, and the designer slumped to the ground, blood from his fatal head wounds pooling on the steps. The killer walked away.

Police promptly launched a nationwide manhunt for their prime suspect, Andrew Cunanan, a 27-year-old gay hustler. Already on the FBI's Ten Most Wanted list, Cunanan was a suspect in four previous murders. Eight days later, the native of San Diego, who'd been an eye-catching presence on the city's gay scene since his teens and was rumored to have AIDS, was found dead on a blue houseboat in Miami Beach, having shot himself in the mouth with a .40-caliber pistol.

Versace, the son of a seamstress and an appliance salesman from southern Italy, designed his first gown at age 9. During his two decades at the epicenter of the design world, he reveled in just the sort of high life Cunanan chased after; indeed, Cunanan boasted to friends that he'd once met Versace at the San Francisco Opera. The designer had opulent tastes and created a residential realm worthy of a Roman emperor. "I can spend $3 million in two hours," he once boasted. Even so, he left behind a fortune estimated at $800 million—large enough to make his principal heir, Allegra, the daughter of Donatella, Versace's sister and creative muse, one of the richest children in the world.

Versace threw lavish parties for such celebrated friends as Raquel Welch, Madonna and Tupac Shakur (top). Sister Donatella (middle) inspired his creations, ran his sprawling empire and will carry on his work. The police cordon (bottom) ran in front of the steps where Versace was slain.

Love of Labour

Britain's new PM is the young, Clintonesque Tony Blair

Long before the May vote that swept the Labour party into office, making Tony Blair, 44, the youngest British prime minister in 185 years, the parallels between the guitar-strumming politician and saxophone-playing Bill Clinton were unmistakable. Like Clinton, Blair is an Oxford-educated liberal who campaigned on traditionally conservative issues; he is married to a prominent lawyer, Cherie Booth, who supported the household (a brood of three) while her husband rose in politics; and he knew economic hardship in his youth. But the stylistic kinship with Clinton became most obvious right after the death of Princess Diana when the media-savvy Blair coached the Queen on how to respond to her public criticism and signaled that he himself felt Britons' pain, felicitously dubbing Diana "the People's Princess."

Jump for Joy

The bearable lightness of being an ex-President

Forced to jump from his disabled Navy bomber in the Pacific during World War II, George Bush promised himself that one day he would try another leap just for fun. The 41st President got the chance at 72, parachuting from 12,500 feet over an Arizona Army facility and landing within 40 yards of his target, as wife Barbara watched. "I'm a new man," he said. "I go home exhilarated."

At her Senate confirmation hearing in January, Albright applauded her three daughters (from left), Katie, Alice and Anne.

Madam Secretary

Taking office as the nation's top diplomat, Madeleine Albright confronted a shrouded past

As a young mother, Madeleine Albright found herself coping with the precarious health of twins born six weeks prematurely. With babies Anne and Alice in incubators, Albright took a crash course in Russian—partly to get her mind off her anxiety. "Then," says Anne, now 36 and a lawyer outside D.C., "once we were fine, she just continued." Her mother now speaks fluent Russian.

Unflappable, pragmatic and determined not to waste a moment—that also described the 60-year-old divorcée who in 1997 became the first woman to serve as U.S. Secretary of State. "She's no shrinking violet," says an ex-colleague from the U.N., where Albright was U.S. ambassador from 1993 to 1996. "She can be biting."

She could also be knocked off balance. As Albright prepared to take office, a reporter researching a profile of her discovered a secret that Albright's parents—who had fled from Czechoslovakia with their children in the late 1930s—had hidden: They had been born Jewish and converted to Catholicism to escape Nazi persecution. And three of Albright's grandparents, about whom she had known little, had perished in Nazi death camps. "This was obviously a major surprise to me," Albright said of her grandparents' fate. Forced to confront the revelations in the public eye, Albright visited a Prague synagogue where her paternal grandparents' names are etched among those of thousands of Czech Holocaust victims. "I leave here tonight," she said, "with the certainty that this new part of my identity adds something stronger, sadder and richer to my life."

Love Bites Back

Marv Albert goes from sin to spin, but the taint, like his weave, may not come off

For NBC sportscaster Marv Albert, his trial on charges of assaulting and sexually forcing himself on Vanessa Perhach, 42, a former mistress, was like a rigged midfield coin flip: Heads he would lose, tails he would lose more. If convicted, Albert, 56, faced upward of five years in prison. If found not guilty, he would still be left with a humiliatingly compromised reputation: His own attorney, Roy Black, was compelled to concede in his opening argument that his client had unconventional sexual preferences, including a taste for rough sex.

Even so, as the trial got under way, the outcome seemed anything but certain. Though rulings by Judge Benjamin Kendrick blocked repeated attempts by Albert's lawyers to introduce evidence challenging

Perhach's credibility and portraying her as emotionally unstable, Black still scored major points. The most damaging came on Day 2, when he played a tape of a conversation in which Perhach appeared to go along with a cab driver's suggestion that he should be rewarded with $50,000 and a new car if he testified that Albert frequently asked him to find "boys" for sex.

Then on Day 3 came the prosecution's stunning surprise: P.J. Masten, a Hyatt Hotels executive, recounted a graphic story of attempted sexual abuse by the broadcaster almost identical to that for which he was being tried. Over strenuous defense objections, Judge Kendrick allowed Masten to describe in riveting detail how Albert had tried to sexually assault her on two occasions. During the second incident, in 1994 in a Dallas hotel room, she claimed a garter-belt-wearing Albert, "exposed and aroused," attacked her before she managed to flee—after yanking off his lumpy chestnut toupee. Masten also offered a steamy play-by-play of the broadcaster's alleged predilections, among them, biting and "threesomes," including male partners.

The morning after Masten's appearance, Team Albert threw in the towel. "Finally it just got to to be too much," said Black. "He worried about how [his family was] dealing with the grinding trial." Albert pleaded guilty to misdemeanor assault-and-battery, and the felony charge of forcible sodomy was dropped. Subsequently, sentencing was suspended for a year while Albert underwent counseling.

A few weeks later, Albert hauled himself off to celebritydom's favorite public confessor, Barbara Walters, and insisted during an interview for ABC's *20/20*, "What happened that night in the hotel is completely a fictitious account. . . . It was all consensual." He maintained that the alleged bites were superficial, "which means they were hickeys," and clarified another issue of great moment: No, he doesn't wear a toupee, it's a hair-weave—and can't be pulled off.

Although Marv Albert (in mugshot and, at left, with fiancée Heather Faulkiner) pled guilty to biting Vanessa Perhach (below) on the back, he later insisted that "no force was involved at all. Never. That's not me."

Despite Albert's immediate sacking by NBC after he pled guilty, all is not lost for the broadcast booth's famous Yesss! man. A poll showed that some 70% of the public thought Albert should be allowed to return to the air, and WFAN, a sports-radio station in New York City floated a job offer. And for all his travail, the divorced Albert had his share of blessings. His four grown children all stuck by his side through the excruciating proceedings, as did his 81-year-old father. So did fiancée Heather Faulkiner, 39, a freelance producer at ESPN, although she admitted to Walters, "I felt like I had just had a stake driven through my heart. I'm still very upset about it."

Fangs a Lot
More tales of al dente offenses

▲ **MIKE TYSON** once again demonstrated his capacity for crossing the line of propriety when he bit off a chunk of Evander Holyfield's right ear, then chomped on his left one during a June heavyweight bout in Las Vegas. While Holyfield took 15 stitches, Tyson took it on the chin: He was banned indefinitely from the ring and was pummeled in the court of public opinion.

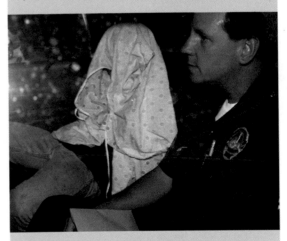

▲ **CHRISTIAN SLATER** topped his own brawling bad-boy image when, police charge, he got into an August fight with a female friend at a party, then sank his incisors into the stomach of a man who came to her defense. The *One Night Stand* star, who had been on a dangerous coke and alcohol binge, was sentenced to 90 days in jail followed by three months in a rehab clinic.

Two Futures on Hold

As two teens await trial on charges of murdering their newborn, their romance cools

To their parents and neighbors in the suburban New Jersey enclave of Wyckoff, Amy Grossberg and Brian Peterson are simply a couple of kids who got into trouble, then made a tragic mistake. That "mistake" involved the death of their newborn son and the depositing of his body in a dumpster outside a Delaware motel in November 1996. "There's enormous support for the couple," says Joyce Harper, owner of a Wyckoff store.

It is unclear, however, if Grossberg and Peterson, both now 19, remain supportive of each other. Though they live just two miles apart, they rarely see each other and speak infrequently. When Grossberg's attorney announced in October that he will file a motion for separate trials for the teenagers, legal experts surmised that Grossberg wants to distance herself from her codefendant—then lay their son's death on him. But that is just speculation, and Grossberg hasn't sat for an extensive interview since her appearance in June on ABC's *20/20*, when, appearing with her parents, Grossberg told Barbara Walters, "I would never hurt anything or anybody, especially something that could come from me."

Peterson and Grossberg might well have escaped detection had Grossberg not collapsed in her University of Delaware dorm in Newark. After paramedics took her to Christiana Hospital, doctors determined that she had given birth to a baby, possibly within the last 12 hours. Only after doctors told Grossberg that the placenta had not yet been expelled from her body did she admit she'd had a baby. Eventually, a police "cadaver" dog found the dead newborn in a gray plastic bag. After an autopsy showed that the infant had been born healthy and had then died as the result of multiple skull fractures and also having been shaken, prosecutors announced that they would be seeking the death penalty.

While the teenagers await their spring 1998 trial, Peterson works in his stepfather's video distribution business and helps coach a youth soccer team; Grossberg is employed at a bakery and does volunteer work at her synagogue. As they go about their business, both have a $300,000 bail hanging over their heads—and black electronic monitoring bands around their ankles.

A Dance Macabre

Charged with killing her baby at the prom, Melissa Drexler faces an uncertain future

After giving birth, Drexler requested a Metallica song, then hit the dance floor with Lewis (above, arriving at the prom).

Until the nightmarish events on June 6 that turned Lacey Township High School's senior prom into a tabloid spectacle, Melissa Drexler was known as a quiet, diligent student—an aspiring fashion designer who dreamed of becoming the next Donna Karan. She seemed shy and opened up to only a few close friends. "When you get to know her, she can be exciting," says Jim Botsacos, 18, a longtime friend. "She likes to have fun." But Drexler concealed more than a desire to enjoy herself. Through most of her senior year, Drexler managed, beneath baggy, loose-fitting clothes, to conceal that she was pregnant. No one knew—not her classmates, not her parents, not even her boyfriend, John Lewis, 20.

The evening of the prom, Drexler arrived with Lewis in a limousine at the Garden Manor in Aberdeen, New Jersey. After she entered the banquet hall in a floor-length, black sleeveless velvet gown, Drexler retreated to the rest room, purportedly to freshen up. She remained there for more than a half hour, eventually moving from one stall to another. Lisa Brewer, a friend who had waited outside, checked on her, at one point noticing blood dripping to the floor and a plastic bag with something in it. Drexler assured Brewer that she was simply having a heavy period.

But soon after Drexler dabbed on some makeup, zipped her dress and returned to the prom, a maintenance worker found a blood-streaked mess in the stalls and a sanitary-napkin dispenser wrenched from the bathroom wall. (Drexler had apparently used its jagged edge to cut the umbilical cord.) Perplexed by a heavy trash bag that had been tied shut, the cleaner had a co-worker carry it outside, where they opened it to discover the body of a 6-lb. 6-oz. baby boy. Confronted on the dance floor by two teachers, Drexler first denied giving birth, then admitted it and was sent by ambulance to a

Though charged with murder, Melissa (with mom Maria and lawyer at arraignment) will not face the death penalty.

nearby hospital, where she delivered the placenta and the baby was declared dead. On October 27, when she was arraigned on murder charges, she pled not guilty.

By all accounts, Drexler's parents, a former bank employee and a computer worker, doted on their only child and indulged her with gifts. "If you can say anything about the parents, they did too much for her," said Debbie Jacobson, the mother of one of Drexler's friends. "She might be 18 chronologically, but emotionally she's definitely not. She wouldn't be prepared to handle this." If it goes to trial (such cases are often settled out of court), the defense is expected to argue either that Drexler, now 19, was suffering a psychological disorder and was acting while in denial of the pregnancy and delivery, or the baby was not alive at birth. Prosecutors have made their position clear: The baby died from manual strangulation and asphyxiation.

The Mother of Modern Comets

Amateur stargazers Alan Hale and Thomas Bopp share a discovery

As the early evening sky turned a pale crimson, Alan Hale and Thomas Bopp stood on a dirt road high in New Mexico's Sacramento Mountains, searching the horizon for signs of a comet—*their* comet—on its route through the solar system. "It's fading in and out," said Hale, peering through binoculars. Moments later, the celestial body was unmistakable—a large, fuzzy splotch of light set off against an array of brightening stars. Officially designated Comet C/1995-01, it is known to the world as Hale-Bopp, after the two amateur astronomers who discovered it, independently, in July 1995: Hale, 39, in New Mexico, and Bopp, 47, in Arizona. Hale-Bopp proved more brilliant than any observed from this planet in 400 years. In late March and early April, the comet, which astronomers calculate made its last visit 4,200 years ago, traveled closest to earth, approaching within 122 million miles. "It looks good," said Bopp, when the two men got together to co-track their co-discovery. Remarkably, there was no hint of rivalry. "His discovery is as legitimate as mine," said Hale of Bopp, who responded, "I think it's neat [Hale] turned out to be a nice guy."

Heady Sojourn

Steering from Earth, Brian Cooper used Mars as his personal freeway

As the designated driver of Sojourner, the little six-wheeled robot that explored the surface of Mars on NASA's Pathfinder Mission, Brian Cooper got to live out the ultimate Nintendo fantasy. "This is what I wanted to do since I came to the Jet Propulsion Laboratory," said Cooper, 37, a 12-year veteran at NASA. "I've always had a fascination for things you can control." Adds his wife Lynne, 36, also an engineer at JPL: "He basically built his own video game. Now he's playing it."

And what a game it was. "I can see the surface of Mars as if I'm standing there," he exulted, donning his special goggles to scout the landscape on his computer screen at JPL in Pasadena. Before beaming directions, Cooper first tried out different routes with a virtual rover at JPL. Then he sent Sojourner on its way—at a non-California speed of 2 feet per minute.

Rocketeer

Keith Hippely's Red Planet Sojourner toy gets into orbit

Scientists will be analyzing the rocks and soil on Mars for years to discover the planet's composition. Mattel execs already know: pay dirt. Captivated by Sojourner's exploration of the Red Planet, kids and collectors sent sales of the company's $5 toy—the Hot Wheels JPL Sojourner Mars Rover—soaring. "I've been with Mattel for 16 years and had some successes but nothing that's generated the excitement this has," says Keith Hippely, 40, who led a five-person team creating the replica, complete with Pathfinder spacecraft, lander and a rover with six-wheel, "rocker-bogie" suspension. Exclaims Hippely: "It was a once-in-a-lifetime thing for a toy designer."

In 1994 members of the Heaven's Gate sect posed on a California beach, brandishing a manifesto that offered "the only way out of this corrupt human kingdom."

Heaven Couldn't Wait

Propelled by visions of a UFO, 39 cultists kill themselves

Though eerie, there might have been something almost reassuring about the image of bug-eyed fanatics ranting about UFOs, the Next Level of existence and the arrival of the comet Hale-Bopp. That, at least, would have conformed to the stereotype of what members of a doomsday cult should be like. But last March following the self-poisoning of 39 members of the Heaven's Gate cult in Rancho Santa Fe, California—the largest mass suicide in U.S. history—stereotypes unraveled quickly. Though some of those who joined Heaven's Gate had obvious emotional problems, most of the 21 women and 18 men, ranging in age from 26 to 72, seemed disarmingly ordinary. They were largely businessmen, mothers and students, who designed home pages for the Internet and seemed consumed by nothing more exotic than a desire for spiritual enlightenment. Leading their quest was Marshall Herff Applewhite, 65, a man whose dream of a career in music had long since been replaced by a confused cosmology of Jesus and UFOs that proved fatally seductive. "Many of these people weren't losers with low self-esteem," says Joan Culpepper, 62, a former advertising executive who was among the first members of the cult in 1975 and later became an outspoken foe. "Applewhite's message connected to some belief in them."

Applewhite, who fought his own homosexuality, submitted to surgical castration, as did seven other sect members.

This screen from the group's Web site depicts a purported being from heaven.

Applewhite was strict about enforcing group discipline. Members had to sign out to get their driver's licenses and car keys before they could leave the compound; there was a seating chart for members when they watched TV; and for a while there was "tomb time," during which members could not speak to each other for days on end. Occasionally tuning forks would be taped to the cultists' heads in an effort to dispel human thoughts. Key to Applewhite's control was a buddy system in which members were assigned partners with whom they were supposed to do everything—eat, work and sleep. To ensure that no one got too friendly or romantically involved, these pairings were rotated regularly. The reign persisted to the end. While Applewhite died alone in the master bedroom, the rest perished in three groups, by first swallowing phenobarbital mixed with applesauce or pudding, then vodka, then placing plastic bags over their heads—all in the blissful belief a spaceship was waiting to carry away their spirits. Comments Culpepper: "I could almost hear them say, 'I'll see you on the spaceship.'"

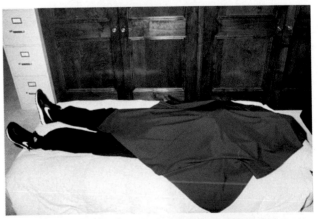

Uniformly clad in black pants, flowing black shirts and brand-new black Nike sneakers, all but the last two members of the cult to die were covered by purple shrouds.

Malcolm posed before his '65 death with Betty and a child.

After the fire, Shabazz was arrested wandering in a daze.

A Dream Ends in Tragedy—Again

Malcolm X's widow, Betty Shabazz, dies in a fire set by her grandson

At the age of 63, Betty Shabazz, widow of Black Muslim leader Malcolm X, lamented the task that lay before her, yet she never flinched from it. Betty's troubled daughter Qubilah Shabazz, who at age 4 had witnessed her father's assassination, seemed unable to raise her own son, 12-year-old Malcolm, named after his martyred grandfather. And so Betty had agreed to provide the youngster with what she'd provided for her own six daughters: a stable home and firm guidance. "She was from that generation," says Ernest Davis, a longtime friend, "that still believed that you have to invest in children and sacrifice for them." For Shabazz, the sacrifice proved too great. Just after midnight on June 1, young Malcolm doused a hallway inside his grandmother's Yonkers, New York, apartment with gasoline, then set it afire. Clad only in a nightgown, Shabazz ran through the flames to escape, suffering third-degree burns over 80 percent of her body. Rushed to a hospital burn unit, she underwent five operations before dying 23 days later. Her death ignited a grief that drew thousands to a Manhattan memorial service to pay tribute to the woman who for 32 years had both toiled tirelessly to preserve her late husband's legacy and carved out her own career as an educator at Medgar Evers College in Brooklyn. Two months after her death, Malcolm, who mental health professionals labeled psychotic and schizophrenic, was sentenced to the maximum 18 months in a juvenile detention center with the possibility of extensions that could keep him locked up until his 18th birthday.

Bittersweet Reunion

Singer Joni Mitchell reunites with the daughter she placed for adoption 32 years ago

At 21, Joni Mitchell was caught in a hell from which there seemed no escape. Single and destitute, her talent as yet undiscovered, the Canadian folksinger was also the new mother of a baby girl. She saw no avenue of support: She had chosen to hide the pregnancy from her parents, and the baby's father, an artist, had long since disappeared. In desperation, Mitchell married a fellow folksinger. But that union quickly collapsed, and Mitchell placed the infant with an adoption agency. Haunted by the loss, Mitchell wrote of her pain ("Child with a child pretending, weary of lies you are sending home") and her hope for the child ("Have a happy ending") in the song "Little Green." Otherwise she hugged her secret tight. Only after a former roommate from the 1960s sold the story of the adoption to a tabloid in 1993 did Mitchell

begin to speak openly, in hopes of reuniting with the girl who had become someone else's daughter at 6 months.

That baby, meanwhile, had grown up happily in a comfortable Toronto suburb as Kilauren Gibb, the daughter of teachers David and Ida Gibb. Fearful of losing their daughter to the birth mother, the Gibbs did not tell Kilauren of the adoption until she was 27. Single and pregnant, Kilauren, a former model, filed an application with a public agency for information about her biological parents. After a frustrating five-year quest, she received a packet that identified her birth mother as a folksinger born in Saskatoon, Saskatchewan, of Norwegian-Scottish descent who had suffered in childhood from polio.

Encouraged by friends who had heard of Mitchell's own search and saw in her face a distinct resemblance, Kilauren dug deeper and hit paydirt on the Internet's Joni Mitchell home page. "There were like 14 or 15 matches," she said of the overlap of information. Two months later, Kilauren flew to Los Angeles with her son, Marlin, 4, to meet Mitchell. "I've had pain and joy in my life, but nothing like this," Mitchell told reporters. "It's an unparalleled emotional feeling."

Mir's Canny Mr. Fixit

Mike Foale's time on the Russian space station tests a can-do astronaut's skills

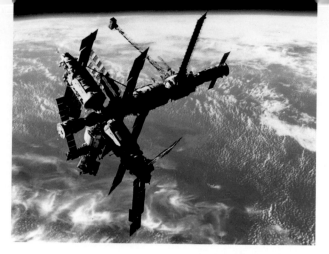

Imagine a trip so jinxed that your vehicle crashes, a fellow traveler develops heart trouble and all your possessions, right down to your toothbrush, are irretrievably lost. Then imagine that you can't turn around and call it quits, because you're 230 miles from home—straight up. So passed the difficult summer of astronaut Michael Foale, the lone American for four months aboard the cramped and battered 11-year-old Russian space station *Mir*—the celestial equivalent of a '65 Pinto.

A low-key computer whiz, avid windsurfer and veteran of three NASA shuttle missions, Foale, 40, was at first teasingly called a CIA spy by his two cosmonaut colleagues. But in the crunch he emerged as one of the most intrepid space explorers this side of Captain Kirk,

coolly handling a series of potentially life-threatening mishaps befitting his nickname at NASA: Mr. Fixit. "Down the line," predicts U.S. shuttle commander Bill Readdy, "Mike will turn out to be one of the big heroes in all of this." Certainly Foale was already a hero to Jenna, 5, and Ian, 2, who sat on a Seabrook, Texas, pier many nights with their mom, Rhonda, 39, a geologist with a master's in space science herself, waving at the *Mir*—and waiting for daddy to come home.

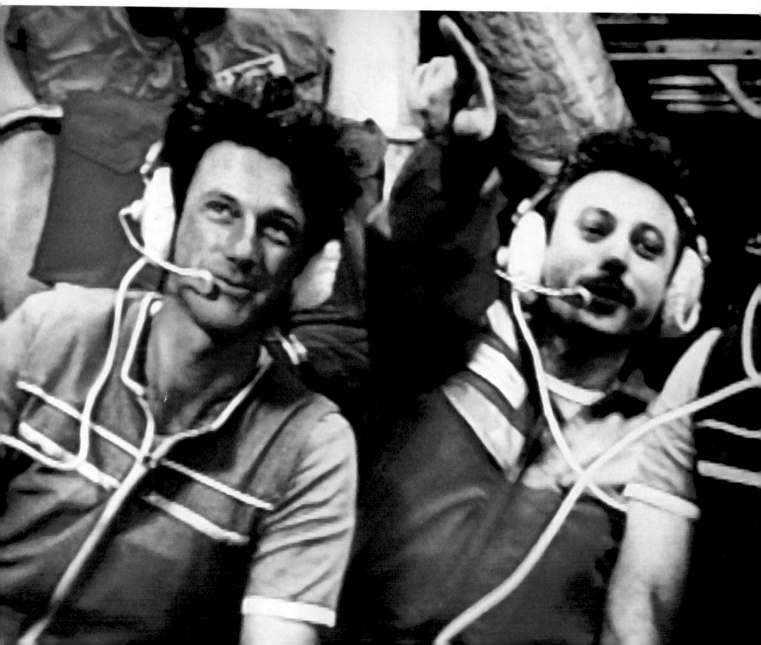

When the *Mir* (top left) collided with an out-of-control resupply ship, losing precious oxygen, Foale (below, left) was ordered by crewmates Aleksandr Lazutkin and Vasily Tsibliev into an escape capsule but instead courageously joined their effort to seal the damage and, in the end, save them all.

Golly, Dolly, That Really Ewe?

A Scottish team clones a lamb and ignites a fiery debate

On February 25, reporters from around the globe flocked to a village near Edinburgh to see its celebrity, a 7-month-old Finn-Dorset lamb named Dolly, who had begun life as a speck of DNA from a female sheep of which she is now a perfect genetic copy. If all the world seemed excited about the first animal to be cloned from an adult, Ian Wilmut, head of the team that created Dolly, was hardly transported by his overnight fame. "You'll all be gone by tomorrow," he said to reporters with a wave of his hand.

The issues raised by Dolly, however, were less dismissible. Until the advent of Dolly, scientists had mostly assumed that cloning mature animals would remain the stuff of science fiction. But Wilmut, 52, and his Roslin Institute researchers proved them wrong and catapulted biogenetics into a future no one seems quite prepared for. Some scientists were exhilarated by the potential for creating, say, a breed of super-productive cows; others worried about *The Boys from Brazil*-type horrors of such genetic engineering. While Wilmut agrees that human-cloning scenarios are "appalling," he prefers to emphasize the positive nature of his colleagues, declaring, "I believe we are a moral species."

Despite his triumph with Dolly (above, left), Ian Wilmut (in his lab) says of himself, "Genius, no. Persistent, yes."

51

Earned Stripes

Woods couldn't win 'em all, but all eyes were on the Tiger

He may be "The Man," but there's still a lot of kid in 21-year-old Tiger Woods. The April night before he ushered in a new era in golf—his own—Woods turned his otherworldly focus on another passion: Mortal Kombat. With the final round of the 61st Masters just hours away, Woods relaxed with buddies in a rented house near Georgia's Augusta National Golf Course and played his favorite video game late into the night. "I told him, 'No basketball,' " says his personal golf coach Butch Harmon. "I didn't want him to jam a finger." The next day Woods blew away the field, finishing with a stunning 270—18 under par for 72 holes, besting by one stroke the tourney record, set in 1965 by Jack Nicklaus. Woods also became the youngest player ever to win the Masters, and the first African-American to take any of golf's four majors. (Augusta National did not even have a black member until 1990.) Two months later at the U.S. Open, Woods tied for 19th but seized the No. 1 spot in the world golf rankings. Then he went into a slight slump, letting down the U.S. side in the Ryder Cup, losing matches that enabled the opposing international team to win by a point. But by the end of his first full year, Woods had emerged as the sport's greatest draw, attracting younger, more diverse galleries even as he occasionally missed a Friday cut. Tiger Woods, super golfer, proved just as engaging now that he was human.

"I accomplished my goal," said Woods, who wept with joy while embracing his father, Earl, moments after his historic Masters win in April; in July, the co-owner danced at the opening of his newest Official All Star Cafe in Miami's South Beach; in August, he showed his frustration after missing a birdie putt during the final round of the Buick Open in Grand Blanc, Michigan, but in the end tied for eighth and took home $43,500.

Unsinkable Sir

Paul McCartney is beknighted, then beheaded by the critics

Once he was known as the Cute Beatle. But in March, the beloved musician and songwriter was knighted by Queen Elizabeth for his service to music. The new Sir Paul McCartney, 54, modestly allowed, "My mum and dad would have been extremely proud." It was a high point in a difficult year that saw McCartney's wife, Linda, 54, fighting breast cancer. Then, in November, McCartney's first symphony, *Standing Stone*, debuted to rotten notices from reviewers who found the work grandiose and repetitive. Nonetheless, the CD, featuring a 300-person orchestra and chorus, shot straight to the top of *Billboard*'s classical chart.

HIZZONER, SO PRETTY IN PINK

In a year in which he won a re-election landslide leading to speculation about higher aspirations, New York City's Rudolph Giuliani, 53, joined Julie Andrews and the Broadway cast of *Victor/Victoria* in the antic annual co-roast of City Hall and its press corps. The normally buttoned-down mayor did a Marilyn Monroe-style send-up, "Happy Birthday, Mr. President—and Regards to Hillary, Too."

Babes in Boyland

Get used to it, guys: Two gutsy women are the NBA's newest referees

The moment Violet Palmer had dreamed about arrived on October 31, when a crowd of 17,021 fans at a National Basketall Association game in Vancouver, British Colombia, serenaded the rookie referee with a chorus of boos for a call against the hometown Grizzlies. Little did they realize that being heckled by fans is music to the ears of both Palmer, 33, and Dee Kantner, 37, the NBA's first female refs. Be warned: Kantner and Palmer, both single, give as good as they get. "Confrontation is part of being a referee," says Palmer. Her hoop skills earned her a scholarship to Cal Poly Pomona, where she led her team to two NCAA Division II titles. Kantner attended the University of Pittsburgh on a field hockey scholarship. In their rookie season, the two will handle only 55 games—and collect $80,000 each.

Says Palmer (with A.C. Green, right) of her and Kantner (above with Doug Brandt): "We've already been accepted."

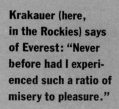

Krakauer (here, in the Rockies) says of Everest: "Never before had I experienced such a ratio of misery to pleasure."

SENSATIONS

Storming the Charts

Author Jon Krakauer's vivid account of a killer blizzard on Mount Everest makes for killer sales

Jon Krakauer's 1996 assault on Nepal's Mount Everest was a brutal struggle against numbing cold and blinding solar radiation that left four members of his climbing party dead, including the leader, after a fierce storm enveloped the summit. Krakauer's assault on the bestseller list was a different matter entirely: Soon after he published his nonfiction narrative of that ascent, *Into Thin Air,* the book climbed to the top of the charts and stayed there. A gripping read, it described in harrowing detail the gale-force collision of bad weather, bad luck and worse judgment that snuffed out a total of 12 lives at once on the world's highest peak. Despite moments of heartbreaking heroism, Krakauer's saga was largely one of hubris and stubbornness. The reading public, meanwhile, still mopping their brows over his Everest tale, installed him concurrently on the paperback Top 10 with his anatomy of another wilderness tragedy, *Into the Wild.* Then, in November, Krakauer got to watch himself, or a more handsome version of himself, scale prime time as ABC telecast a melodramatic movie adaptation of *Into Thin Air.*

The 43-year-old writer, however, has had a hard time accepting his good luck and has often found himself a bit sleepless in his Seattle home. Already plagued with survivor's guilt, he has also had to contend with charges that he is profiting from his fellow climbers' tragedy. "It's hard when a widow calls you up at 2 a.m. and accuses you of selling her loved one's name," he says. "Before Everest, I'd never even been to a funeral." An accomplished mountaineer, Krakauer had promised to quit the dangerous sport when he got married in 1980. Though his marriage almost broke up over the issue, he couldn't kick the habit. When *Outside* magazine offered him the chance to realize his years-long dream, he leapt at the assignment. "Now," says Krakauer, "I wish I'd never heard of Everest."

ONE IF BY LAND, $$$ IF BY SEA

Sebastian Junger, 35, was a struggling nature writer who had to work on the side as a tree cutter, and even his agent was pessimistic about his first book. But *The Perfect Storm,* which tells the stories of six men who went down in a Gloucester, Massachusetts, fishing boat during a hellacious 1991 squall, sailed into best-sellerdom. Junger, who moved to New York City, purchased a 25-foot sloop with his newfound wealth.

Better than knocking
wood was knocking Oscar
heads after Frances Mc-
Dormand and hubby Joel
Coen (in glasses) both
won, she for her perfor-
mance in *Fargo*, he for his
screenplay. Her costar
Steve Buscemi (left)
lent a hand.

Hey, This Guy Is *Really* Funny!

Cruising for miscreant aliens, *Men in Black* star Will Smith proves he's more than a one-megahit Hollywood wonder

In a short and sweet 98 minutes, *Men in Black* proved the runaway Hollywood hit of the summer. The deadpan-funny chase of intergalactic warriors by a pair of top-secret federal agents grossed $235 million domestically, another $128 million overseas. For Will Smith, 29, who had already proved his appeal as a good-natured rapper and amiable sitcom headliner on *Fresh Prince of Bel Air*, the success meant that the previous summer's megahit *Independence Day* was no fluke and that he belonged in the pantheon of top-draw action-hero actors with costar Tommy Lee Jones. *Men in Black* defined not only hot box office but also cool fashion as all America seemed to affect the stars' wraparound Ray-Ban sunglasses, beginning at the premiere party (above) with his son Willard C. III (or "Trey"), 5, and nephew Kyle, 7. In his other breakthrough of the year, Smith, who was divorced from the boy's mother, decided to marry his live-in (and pregnant) lady, actress Jada Pinkett, 26. Professionally a team as well, the couple sold a script called *Love for Hire* to Imagine's Brian Grazer, who believes Smith has now emerged as "one of the biggest stars in the world."

Sweet 16

Martina Hingis slays with a big smile and a lethal racquet

The TV director is having a crisis. On a court in Hilton Head, South Carolina, Martina Hingis is filming a tennis promo for NBC. She just doesn't get it. Joyfully, a huge grin lighting her face, she's whipping ball after ball over the net. But the director wants drama, menace, fury. "No, no, no! You look too happy out there," he shouts. "Make it look harder."

No can do. The kid is a natural—at 16 she's the youngest No. 1 ranked woman this century. Moreover, she plays the game with exhilarating joie de vivre, not to mention unshakable self-confidence. Her 1997 record of 63-2, which included three Grand Slam victories, is the fifth-best one year mark in the history of women's tennis. "Usually at 16 you have great groundies or a great serve-volley, but you don't have the whole package," says tennis legend Chris Evert. "She does."

It's a game Hingis seemed destined to play. Born in what is now Slovakia, Martina, an only child, was named by her Czech tennis-playing parents for their country's greatest champion, Martina Navratilova. At 2 she was already trying to hit balls back to her mother, Melanie Molitor, the only coach she has ever had. By 6, Hingis had won her first tournament. That year Hingis's parents divorced. Soon after, she moved with her mother and new stepfather (another marriage that ended in divorce) to Switzerland. After winning a string of junior Grand Slam titles, she turned pro at 14.

Her only real rough patch came during her first year on the tour, when Hingis struggled with both a weak serve and adolescent rebellion. Eventually, Molitor, whom tennis insiders praise for working Hingis but not driving her, drew a line: Buckle down or go back to school. The result has rewritten the history of tennis.

Golden Glow

Just 15 and a mere 4'10", Tara Lipinski has the edge in the slippery world of women's skating

Though technically brilliant she was artistically immature and regarded as more of a comer than a contender. But at 14, Tara Lipinski, all 4'8¾" and 74 lbs. of her, stunned skating fans by snatching the U.S. national title from veteran Michelle Kwan in February, then proved it was no fluke a month later by taking the world crown. That made her the youngest-ever women's international champion and, given her tender age, a likely force for two or even three Olympiads.

By the end of her amazing year, Lipinski had turned 15 and added 8 lbs. and 1¼ inches to her frame without sacrificing her toothy grin and precocious poise. She skated in some 52 shows, published an autobiography, established a Web site—all the while maintaining a strict daily schedule of four hours hitting the ice and four hours hitting the books. "She's going to college," vows her mother Pat. "She promised me." But the disruptions in her life since taking to the ice at age 6 (she began roller-skating lessons at 3) have not always been easy. To train with coach Richard Callaghan she and her mother had to move to Michigan. The family, says father Jack, a corporate executive who continues to live in Texas, chats twice daily, running up monthly phone bills "of a couple of hundred dollars." Though they hate being separated, neither parent will consider the common skating practice of letting their child live with a host family in Michigan. "We would never do that," says Jack. "We have one daughter, and she's going to be raised by one of us."

Macho Ham

Howard Stern drops his pants to reveal . . . his inner child

Radio shock jock Howard Stern is a human whoopee cushion. What he does isn't polite or correct, but it does make you laugh—which is exactly what fans did in lucrative droves to see Stern star as himself in *Private Parts.* Based on the dee-jay's bestselling 1993 autobiography, the film bares not only Stern's buttocks but also his off-mike insecurities. Most appealing, it showed that, for all his raunchy talk, he is a touchingly devoted family man.

The Graduate

Dropout Matt Lauer is now a Bachelor in two senses

In 1979, when Matt Lauer was 21 and just four credits shy of a bachelor of science degree from Ohio University, WOWK-TV, the West Virginia station where he had interned his senior year, made him an enticing offer: to produce its noon newscast. "I decided a bird in the hand was worth four credits," he recalls. Long after the bird turned into the NBC peacock, where Lauer now serves as coanchor of the *Today* show, he determined to finish what he began so long ago. He struck a bargain with O.U. to write a letter detailing his 18 years in TV to make up the credit shortfall. The letter completed, TV's most eligible morning man delivered O.U.'s commencement speech, then took his place with the Class of '97 to receive his sheepskin.

Much Ado

Ellen DeGeneres comes out, speaks out and stays out

As only the media-deprived can fail to know, Ellen DeGeneres, 39, came out of the closet in 1997—big-time. First she announced on the cover of TIME, "Yep, I'm gay." Then, her alter ego on the middling ABC sitcom *Ellen* realized, in a special one-hour episode in April, that she is not Lebanese—as Degeneres had been joking for months—but lesbian. That was followed by real-life Ellen's disclosure that she was in a serious relationship (yep, with a woman), "something I want to last forever."

After actress Anne Heche, 27, identified herself as the significant other, the two paraded their status as the first Hollywood stars to engage in an openly gay romance. At Washington's annual White House Correspondents' Dinner in late April they embraced during the Pledge of Allegiance, held hands through the smoked-duck-and-mango appetizer and nuzzled through the entrée. "I had the impression they were putting on some kind of act," said a capital columnist. "But this kind of thing can backfire in Washington."

And elsewhere. Rumors that the two wanted to have a baby competed with reports that they were on the rocks. Meanwhile, with the TV Ellen flaunting her gay pride, ABC added a TV-14 rating, meaning the material "might be inappropriate for children under 14." Incensed, Degeneres threatened to quit the comedy. The show went on, and the jury's still out—just like both Ellens.

After Degeneres broke a prime-time taboo by locking lips with Laura Dern on the coming-out episode of *Ellen,* she and companion Heche made the scene.

▲ *3RD ROCK FROM THE SUN* may have an improvised feel, but every buffoonish line and antic move is carefully rehearsed by its ensemble cast of off-the-inanity-charts aliens (from left: John Lithgow, Joseph Gordon-Levitt, Kristen Johnston and French Stewart). For daring in the show's second season on NBC to continue to go where no aliens have gone before, both Lithgow and Johnston picked up Emmys.

49TH ANNUAL PRIME-TIME EMMY AWARDS

(Presented September 14, 1997)
Drama Series: *Law & Order*
Comedy Series: *Frasier*
Variety, Music or Comedy Series: *Tracey Takes On . . .*
Miniseries: *Prime Suspect 5: Errors of Judgement*
Lead Actor, Drama Series: Dennis Franz, *NYPD Blue*
Lead Actress, Drama Series: Gillian Anderson, *The X-Files*
Lead Actor, Comedy Series: John Lithgow, *3rd Rock from the Sun*
Lead Actress, Comedy Series: Helen Hunt, *Mad About You*
Lead Actor, Miniseries or Special: Armand Assante, *Gotti*

Lead Actress, Miniseries or Special: Alfre Woodard, *Miss Evers' Boys*
Supporting Actor, Drama: Hector Elizondo, *Chicago Hope*
Supporting Actress, Drama: Kim Delaney, *N.Y.P.D. Blue*
Supporting Actor, Comedy Series: Michael Richards, *Seinfeld*
Supporting Actress, Comedy Series: Kristen Johnston, *3rd Rock from the Sun*
Supporting Actor, Miniseries or Special: Beau Bridges, *The Second Civil War*
Supporting Actress, Miniseries or Special: Diana Rigg, *Rebecca*
Individual Performance, Variety or Music Show: Bette Midler, *Bette Midler: Diva Las Vegas*

Mr. Average Guy—Not!

Drew Carey dines out on the daily woes of Joe Lout

With his nerdy black-rimmed glasses and bring-on-the-bacon girth, he remains the poster boy for average guys everywhere. But stand-up comedian Drew Carey is hardly one of them anymore. Take his prime-time sitcom, with its weekly send-up of the foibles of Midwestern working stiffs. Now in its third season, the show has found a home in the Nielsen Top 20, a sure sign that he'll last out his five-year contract with ABC. Then, there's his book, *Dirty Jokes and Beer,* subtitled "Stories of the Unrefined." Carey's approach to authorship may have been ordinary enough: He studied how-to tomes from Writer's Digest Books before attempting to weave together his collection of jokes, personal history (including a brief mention of being molested at 9) and essays. But average guys don't get $3 million advances without a ghost; they also don't land on bestseller lists.

So, what remains in the life of Cleveland's favorite son that average mortals might relate to, beyond his preference to chow down at Bob's Big Boy? Well, there is his arsenal of two 9-mm handguns and two assault rifles. "If someone breaks into my house," the ex-Marine told a reporter, "I'm not going to dial 911 and wait for the police." His take on taxes—"unfair"—also strikes a familiar chord. And his bouts with depression undoubtedly resonate, if not his two attempts to kill himself. As for fame and fortune, he seems refreshingly unseduced by the bright lights. "I see fulfilling my five-year contract and disappearing," says the 39-year-old bachelor. "I want to grow a beard, have money and retire. Meanwhile I'm gonna have fun."

The summer's hottest concert ticket was the all-female Lilith Fair tour, a seven-week, 35-city blow-out that featured a rotating cast of rock, country and blues stars, including (clockwise from top) Joan Osborne, Sarah McLachlan, Grammy winner Sheryl Crow and Fiona Apple.

Gilding her Lilith year, Jewel won an unprecedented $2 million contract from HarperCollins to deliver a memoir and a book of poems.

Rare Gem

Naive but knowing, the vagabond Jewel gleams

Three years ago, Jewel Kilcher, now 23, was living in the back of her used VW van and subsisting on carrots and peanut butter just so she could bring her bittersweet songs of unrequited love to San Diego's Innerchange coffeehouse. "I told myself, 'Okay,'" she recalls, "'I'm going to do something I love, or I'm going to die.'" That was before her debut album, 1995's *Pieces of You,* landed in the *Billboard* Top 10. With the reissue of the album this year, compounded by her performances with the Lilith Fair tour and her fetching videos, the fey songstress has become the sextuple-platinum jewel in the folk-rock crown.

Raised in a log cabin on an 800-acre farm near Homer, Alaska, she began performing with her folksinger father after her parents split up. While waitressing at another coffee shop, she met musician Steve Poltz, who became her lover, mentor and co-writer. "I was a social misfit," Jewel says. "I hadn't even heard the Beatles before I met him." Though her romance with Poltz went south, Jewel's career rockets northward.

31ST ANNUAL COUNTRY MUSIC AWARDS

(Presented September 24, 1997)
Entertainer of the Year: Garth Brooks
Male Vocalist: George Strait
Female Vocalist: Trisha Yearwood
Single: "Strawberry Wine," Deana Carter
Album: *Carrying Your Love with Me,* George Strait
Vocal Group: Diamond Rio
Vocal Duo: Brooks & Dunn
Music Video: Kathy Mattea, "455 Rockett"
Horizon Award: LeAnn Rimes
Song: "Strawberry Wine," Matraca Berg, Gary Harrison
Event: Tim McGraw (with Faith Hill), "It's Your Love"

Actual Boys in the Band

Oklahoma's Hanson brothers 'MMMBop' their way to the top

Three pint-size boys from Tulsa approached music attorney Christopher Sabec three years ago as he was munching barbecue in Texas. "Excuse me, sir," they asked. "May we perform for you?" Not wanting to crush their young psyches, he grudgingly agreed. "I need to speak to your parents," Sabec excitedly told them as the last note faded. He quickly signed drummer Zachary, now 11, keyboardist Taylor, 14, and guitarist Isaac Hanson, 16, and sent a demo of their bubbly soul-pop to hundreds of scouts. Intrigued, Mercury Records talent hunter Steve Greenberg tracked the Hansons to a country fair in Kansas. Soon their first album, *Middle of Nowhere,* hit the Top 10, and their single, "MMMBop," went to No. 1 in the U.S. and Europe. Schooled at home with three younger siblings by their mother, Diane, a former professional singer, and their father, Walker, a CPA and an amateur guitarist, the boys are as ingenuous as their sound. The despair of grunge, for instance, they just don't get. "If music is what you do, and you love it," asks Taylor, "why would you be sad?"

Wholesome heartthrobs (from left) Zac, Isaac and Taylor don't see music as a racket.

Abfab with a beat (clockwise from top left): Melanie "Scary Spice" Brown, Emma Lee "Baby Spice" Bunton, Melanie "Sporty Spice" Chisholm, Geri "Ginger Spice" Halliwell, Victoria "Posh Spice" Adams.

Piquant Fliers

Self-styled pop tarts, England's Spice Girls add relish to the charts and the Internet

The Spice Girls admit their talents are limited. "We don't claim to be soul divas," says Melanie Brown, known as Scary Spice for her pierced tongue. Like her mates—modestly successful dancers, actresses or models before they answered an ad in 1994—Brown compensates for artistic shortfall with sass, flash and "girl power" chatter. Not only have the five Brits, who range in age from 21 to 24, sold 10 million copies of their debut album, *Spice*, but they have No. 1 singles in 51 countries, an authorized biography, *Girl Power!*, and a film due in January 1998. All without having given a single concert. But fans, who tap by the millions into the 100,000-odd Spice Girls documents on the Internet, think the quintet totally rad. Many are a tad young. Says Emma Lee "Baby Spice" Bunton, 21, "I get the little boys asking if I can baby-sit."

Radio's Chide Guide

Dr. Laura Schlessinger keeps people listening by telling them what they don't want to hear

The titles of her bestselling books read like a shopping list for a supermarket of dysfunctional behavior: *Ten Stupid Things Women Do to Mess Up Their Lives, Ten Stupid Things Men Do to Mess Up Their Lives*. By satisfying the American appetite for guidance in bite-size bits with no sugarcoating, Dr. Laura, as her fans know her, has emerged as the nation's top radio therapist. On a call-in program heard daily by 18 million listeners on some 430 stations—her ratings are second only to Rush Limbaugh's—she combines a dulcet voice with probing questions and slingshot prescriptions as confident as

they are consistent: Don't whine; don't consider yourself a victim; take responsibility; face facts; act morally.

Schlessinger's tough love derives from her own hard road. Her mother was a troubled woman who "blamed everyone else for her unhappiness," says Schlessinger, who describes her father as verbally and even physically abusive. Young Laura retreated to her studies, eventually earning a Ph.D. in physiology. As a recent divorcée in 1979, she called a Los Angeles talk station to answer the question: "Would you rather be a divorcée or a widow?" Her frank response—"A widow. You don't feel guilty. Everybody feels sorry for you"—led to a regular guest spot and then her own show. "I discovered I had a talent for clarifying people's subconscious needs," says Schlessinger, 50, married since 1984 to Dr. Lew Bishop, a former professor of neurophysiology, with whom she has one son, Deryk, 11. "I do not see it as my mission to make anybody feel better. I want them to get better."

Chip Witched

An unflappable supercomputer leaves the chess champ feeling Deep Blue

When world chess champion Garry Kasparov lost less than graciously to the IBM RS/6000 SP supercomputer Deep Blue in a much-hyped May match in Manhattan, it threw some commentators into a tizzy. After all, if a computer can beat the greatest chess player of all time, they reasoned, how long can it be before one, say, launches all the missiles in the world or gets its own late-night talk show? None of the five scientists on the IBM team that programmed the $2 million, 1.4-ton Deep Blue—giving it the power to analyze 200 million chess moves per second—seems worried. "The machine is just a machine to us," says team leader C.J. Tan. "People give it more meaning than we do."

And computer people aren't to be confused with sports fans. After the soreheaded Kasparov resigned in the final game, the IBM-ers had a quiet dinner. No high fives. No dancing in the end zone. They didn't need to. As Joel Benjamin, a chess grandmaster who helped machine beat man, said earlier, "It's Dr. Deep Blue now."

ARTHUR MAKES BARNEY LOOK LIKE A DINOSAUR

What, you may ask, *is* he? A mouse? A squirrel? Well, as any 4-year-old can tell you, Arthur is an aardvark. And as any financial analyst can tell you, he is pure gold. Since 1976, when the amiable aardvark debuted in author Marc Brown's first kids' book, 10 million Arthur volumes have been sold. Last spring, Brown landed a seven-figure advance for books 24 through 27 in the series. What's more, the animated *Arthur,* wrestling with issues like a first pair of glasses or the arrival of a baby sister, has eclipsed a certain saccharine purple dino as PBS's No. 1 kids' show. "Kids can relate to Arthur," says Brown, "because he's dealing with the same problems they are."

From Ashes To Riches

With candor and humor, Frank McCourt spins gold out of his impoverished Irish past

Back when he was teaching English at New York City's Stuyvesant High School, Frank McCourt would urge his students to follow the cardinal rule of writing: Use what you know. The kids, spellbound by their teacher's accounts of his own achingly poor Irish past, would tell him, "Our lives are boring. Your childhood was interesting," recalls McCourt. "They were envious of my misery."

Now they can marvel at his success. At 66, McCourt published a memoir filled with his strikingly unembittered tales of growing up in Limerick in "one of the juiciest slums this side of Bombay." The title, *Angela's Ashes,* honors his late mother, and the book, his first (McCourt felt he couldn't write it in her lifetime), became the U.S.'s No. 1 nonfiction bestseller and won a Pulitzer, though it offended many back in Limerick. "My dream was to have a Library of Congress catalog number, that's all," says McCourt, who retired from teaching in 1987 and lives with his third wife, a publicist, in a Manhattan apartment.

Born in Brooklyn to recent-immigrant parents, McCourt was 4 when his laborer father, unable to tough out the Depression, moved the family back to Ireland. But the family fared no better in Limerick. Over the years, McCourt saw three of six siblings die before they were 3 and watched his father drink away the dole money they needed for food. "We were below welfare," he says. "We begged from people on welfare." McCourt will never face such hardship again: He earned $1 million for the paperback rights to his memoir and another six-figure sum for the movie rights.

Major Leaguer

Sheryl Swoopes helps birth a boy—and a female NBA

Sheryl Swoopes was just 7 years old when she first challenged her two older brothers on the gravel basketball court they'd fashioned in the front yard of their home in the tumbleweed town of Brownfield, Texas. The boys dribbled around her, called her names, and predicted she would quit. Instead, Swoopes joined the Little Dribblers, a league for girls, and quickly proved to be a standout. Her high school's player of the year, Swoopes went on to become the star of the nation's top college team at Texas Tech University, scoring 47 points in the 1993 NCAA title game. Undeterred by her failure to make the 1992 Olympic team, the 6', 145-lb. Swoopes qualified four years later and was key to the dazzling play that clinched the gold medal and convinced Americans that female hoop stars deserved a league of their own. Post-Atlanta, Swoopes, 26, signed with the Houston Comets, then had to sit out the first half of the premiere season of the Women's National Basketball Association while she and her husband, Eric Jackson, 23, awaited their first child, Jordan Eric, who entered their starting lineup June 25.

Shine in the Glare

Panned by critics but embraced by fans, pianist David Helfgott tremulously tours

While on the road, Australian pianist David Helfgott wanted to hug everyone. At a New York City reception celebrating his and his wife's arrival for a much-anticipated U.S. concert tour, the lanky 49-year-old musician grabbed a virtual stranger, wrapped him in a bear hug, then invited him to the piano. "Keep smiling," he murmured as he began playing. "It's a miracle. Have you seen the film? It's the greatest movie ever made. Oh-ho! I'm very, very lucky."

In some ways Helfgott certainly is. Despite a decades-long battle with what doctors describe as a "schizoaffective disorder," he managed to function well enough to complete a sold-out tour of 11 cities. What's more, the low-budget Australian movie *Shine,* which chronicles Helfgott's journey from child prodigy to emotional wreck, grossed more than $30 million ➤

in the U.S. and earned Helfgott's portrayer, Geoffrey Rush, who once suffered a brief mental breakdown himself, an Academy Award. Helfgott's recording of Rachmaninoff's Piano Concerto No. 3 (the "Rach 3" that prompts his breakdown in the film) soared to the top of classical charts on three continents. And wherever Helfgott played, fans responded with thundering ovations and rushed to the stage to touch him. "It's like we've been attached to a very friendly rocket and put into orbit," says his wife, Gillian, 65, whose book *Love You to Bits and Pieces: My Life with David Helfgott* has sold briskly.

David and Gillian Helfgott (poolside in Sydney) are as ebullient a couple in real life as they seem in *Shine*, a film that prompted the pianist to brave the concert stage again (above left). *Shine* costars Geoffrey Rush and Lynn Redgrave met with Helfgott (center) in 1995.

But what might have been a purely jubilant comeback tour became something that looked, from certain angles, like a disaster. While audiences loved him, critics panned Helfgott's performances for his sloppy technique, thin tone and distracting habit of talking and singing to himself onstage. "He is not a finished performer in any sense," warned *The New York Times*. Some observers slammed Gillian and greedy promoters for exploiting the emotionally fragile artist. And others, including some of Helfgott's siblings, questioned the film's accuracy—particularly the sections that suggested Helfgott's late father, Peter, had abused his children physically as well as emotionally. "The film is brilliant, but it's not factual," said younger brother Leslie, a violinist. "My father was not a brutal person."

Helfgott's opinion about the fuss remains a mystery. He declined to give interviews, leaving Gillian to do the talking. Clearly, though, he relished the spotlight. Performing in America had been a particular dream since he was 14, when his father denied him the chance to study in the U.S. on a scholarship. "David has gradually gained a greater sense of wholeness," says Gillian. "I doubt he'll ever be as we would say other people are. But there has been a flowering of him."

WHEN IRISH LEGS ARE KICKING

At the 1994 Eurovision song competition in Dublin, the tune wasn't even on the program—it was played at intermission. But today, "Riverdance" is the title piece of a Gael-force folk-dancing hit. "People are looking for something spiritual, soulful and rooted," says *Riverdance* composer Bill Whelan. "This is a celebration of human connection." Based on traditional Irish step dancing—in which the upper body remains still while legs and feet fly—the show, with its dozens of whirling dancers, has played to packed houses in the U.S. and Australia. And its Grammy-winning soundtrack has jigged for more than a year on *Billboard's* World Music charts.

A Seductive Savage

As a royal barbarian, Lucy Lawless wields a dazzling dual edge: her cleaver and cleavage

"Who could have expected this kind of success?" gushes New Zealander Lucy Lawless, 29, about her astral trajectory as *Xena: Warrior Princess*, history's most bodacious barbarian. "My daughter [Daisy, 9] tries to pretend that Mom being Xena is a bit of a burden," says the 5'11" syndicated TV sensation. "But I think she truly loves it." So do the millions of devotees in more than 50 countries where the show airs. "People are attracted to her masculine bent," says Lawless. "Finally, a woman you can have

a beer with." For her convincing portrayal of the leather-clad heroine, a sword-brandishing twist on *Sheena, Queen of the Jungle,* Lawless was hailed by *Ms.* magazine as a feminist icon of the '90s.

The stunning beauty undoubtedly earned new fans last spring when, after delivering a respectful rendition of "The Star-Spangled Banner" at a Mighty Ducks hockey game in California, she raised her arm in an enthusiastic salute—and unwittingly popped out of the skimpy breastplate covering her torso. "Obviously, I was mortified," the good-natured Lawless told reporters. "It was quite a bit more exposure than I want." The debacle apparently didn't put off Robert Tapert, 42, executive producer of both the *Xena* and *Hercules* TV series. In October, Lawless and Tapert announced their engagement. It will be Lawless's second trip to the altar, and Tapert's first.

'97's Sexiest Man Alive

PEOPLE's choice cut of beef is heartstoppingly handsome, funny and—catch this—nice, too

Damn, he makes it look easy. He just tilts his head, dips his chin, drops his eyes—then, wham!—back up come the eyes, full of mischief and magic, atop a sly half grin that teases, "Yep, I'm trouble, but you love me anyway." And do fans ever. Whether he's playing doctor in the *ER*, battling supervillains in *Batman & Robin* or chasing down stolen nukes in *Peacemaker*, George Clooney, 36, has jump-started more hearts than a whole fleet of defibrillators. "There's something that women call being a real guy," says Lynda Obst, producer of his movie *One Fine Day*. "He's it." Clooney, the real guy, is known for his zany sense of humor and near-legendary loyalty to friends. "My boyfriend always says, 'He can't be that nice,' " says actress Christa Miller, who also shoots on the Warner lot. "And I just say, 'He *is* that nice.' " And handsome, too. Damn.

PEOPLE'S 25 MOST INTRIGUING LIST OF 1997

Madeleine Albright, *60, Secretary of State*
Beck, *27, singer*
Drew Carey, *39, comedian*
Bill Clinton, *51, President*
Bill Cosby, *60, comedian*
Andrew Cunanan, *28, serial killer*
Ellen DeGeneres, *39, comedian*
Diana, Princess of Wales, *36*
Leonardo DiCaprio, *23, actor*
Dolly, *cloned sheep*
Kathie Lee Gifford, *44, TV host*
Rudolph Giuliani, *53, New York City Mayor*
Joseph Hartzler, *47, Oklahoma City bombing prosecutor*
Tommy Hilfiger, *46, fashion designer*

Brenda Hoster, *40, whistle-blower on sexual harassment in the Army*
Jewel, *23, singer*
Elton John, *50, singer*
John F. Kennedy Jr., *37, magazine editor*
Lucy Lawless, *29, actress*
Bill McCartney, *57, Promise Keepers leader*
Bobbi McCaughey, *29, mother of all mothers*
Frank McCourt, *66, author*
Michael Moore, *45, scourge of the tobacco industry*
Julia Roberts, *30, actress*
Sheryl Swoopes, *26, women's pro basketball star*

Captain America

Tommy Hilfiger makes waves mixing street audacity with yacht club cool

In 1985, fashion wannabe Tommy Hilfiger launched one of the cheekiest marketing campaigns in Seventh Avenue memory with a teaser billboard in Times Square that cryptically declared, "The 4 Great American Designers for Men are: R _ _ _ L _ _ _ _ _, P _ _ _ E _ _ _ _, C _ _ _ _ _ K _ _ _ _, T _ _ _ _ H _ _ _ _ _ _ _." In almost no time, Hilfiger, an upstart from Elmira, New York, delivered on that hype, becoming the man of the moment in prep-smart sportswear, and now, 12

STYLE

years later, the fashion prince has tirelessly self-promoted his empire to expected annual sales of $2 billion.

In 1997, Hilfiger, 46, opened his first megastore on Beverly Hills' chic Rodeo Drive; he published *All American: A Style Book;* and spread into women's and kids' wear. Next come toiletries and his first home line, including furniture. Though the teenagers who wear his primary-hued, patriotic-themed threads are probably the best advertisement (except for President Clinton, who occasionally dons a Hilfiger tie),

America's hottest clothier leaves nothing to chance. He is constantly on MTV to hold onto his youth franchise, whom he first entranced by dressing rapper Snoop Doggy Dogg. To reach a paunchier audience, he schmoozes with *Playboy.*

Critics harrumph that Hilfiger, who lives in a 22-room Greenwich, Connecticut, farmhouse with his wife and four kids, is more original as a hustler than as a designer. But no rival can match his cross-cultural appeal from inner city to campus to country club.

He hangs with Mariah Carey at a Manhattan benefit.

Fugee Wyclef Jean flashes the TH look on tour.

Skipper of his own fate and ever-more-fabulous fortune, Hilfiger pilots *Miss Ally,* his 35-ft. Hacker Craft, on Long Island Sound.

Penny Marshall shows her loyalty at another N.Y. bash.

NIKKI SIXX of Mötley Crüe

Soul Splotch

A look reminds that hair can be singular as well as plural

BILLY BOB THORNTON

No, these men don't shave in the dark. In fact, their "soul patches," the latest in facial topiary, are deliberate fashion statements. Actor Eric Stoltz, Seattle Mariners pitcher Randy Johnson and the chin-dividuals on this page are just a few of the cool dudes picking up where Gen. George Armstrong Custer and Flemish master Anthony Van Dyck left off. "I wear it because the girls like it," says rocker Sammy Hagar. "I call it the love patch."

Perhaps the style (also known as spits, skids or flavor-savers) became the rage because it's easy come, easy grow. Worn wispy or wide, with or without a mustache, the miniwhiskers go best with "shorter hair, a close, cropped cut," says Jim Wayne, who owns a hair salon by that name in Beverly Hills. "They're great with balding men; it balances it out a bit." And what's next? "Fu Manchu is on the way, I swear," vows Wayne. "It'll be, like, very Village People."

KEANU REEVES

SAMMY HAGAR

VING RHAMES

DAVID BOWIE

JOSH BROLIN

A Pocketful of Miracles

Virtual pets and Beanie Babies turn teenie toys into big bucks

Fuzzy, they ain't. Cute? Depends on your definition. Addictive? You bet. The Tamagotchi beep-beeped its way into fad history in 1997, alongside the Hula Hoop, Rubik's Cube and the Cabbage Patch Doll but in a smaller package. Purchasers become, in effect, parents to these egg-size "virtual pets" on a key chain. Once "hatched" onto a Tamagotchi's tiny screen, a jelly-bean-size critter starts chirping for attention. The owner must push buttons to feed his or her pet, play with it, discipline it, even scoop up after its droppings. If ignored, the tyrannical Tamagotchi (a Japanese word meaning lovable egg) turns cranky and sickly. The record life span is reportedly 83 days. But miscreant "parents" needn't mourn; a new creature hatches at the touch of a reset button. By late 1997 the U.S. population of Tamagotchis (retailing for around $15 each) had mushroomed to 4.5 million. Pretty soon they'll have their own political action committee. But virtual pets were not alone in swamping the market for adorables. New Beanie Baby characters—those pint-size, pastel-colored stuffed animals with soft heads, floppy ears and squishy bodies that made their debut in 1994—continued to skip out of stores at $5 each. But scarcity was the real story. Periodically, Chicago-based Ty, Inc. "retires" some Beanies and introduces new ones. The disappeared dolls reappear with a vengeance on the adult collectibles market, fetching from $25 for '97 retirees to as much as $2,995 for the rare blue 1995 evaporee Peanut the Elephant (left).

ROMA DOWNEY

With her heavenly complexion and cascading auburn hair, *Touched by an Angel's* Roma Downey certainly looks divine. But John Dye, who plays fellow CBS angel Andrew, says his Irish-bred costar has the soul of an angel as well. "It's her glow that makes her really beautiful," he declares. "She still has that little-girl demureness."

The Beauties

Fresh is the word for this year's PEOPLE 50

THE 50 MOST BEAUTIFUL PEOPLE OF 1997

Gillian Anderson, *28, actress*
Lauren Bacall, *72, actress*
David Baldacci, *37, lawyer-author*
Jacinda Barrett, *24, model*
Drew Barrymore, *22, actress*
Juliette Binoche, *33, actress*
Toni Braxton, *29, singer*
Andre Braugher, *34, actor*
Jim Carrey, *35, actor*
Deana Carter, *31, singer*
David Chokachi, *29, actor*
Tom Cruise, *34, actor*
Christopher Cuomo, *26, lawyer*
Claire Danes, *18, actress*
Leonardo DiCaprio, *22, actor*
Oscar De La Hoya, *24, boxer*
Roma Downey, *34, actress*
Michael Flatley, *38, dancer*
Harrison Ford, *54, actor*
Tom Ford, *35, fashion designer*
Vivica A. Fox, *32, actress*
Cuba Gooding Jr., *29, actor*
Jeff Gordon, *25, NASCAR racer*
Mia Hamm, *25, Olympic athlete*

Derek Jeter, *22, baseball player*
Lisa Kudrow, *33, actress*
Matt Lauer, *39, Today show host*
Lucy Lawless, *29, actress*
Jared Leto, *25, actor*
Jennifer Lopez, *26, actress*
Pattie Maes, *35, media professor*
Marie-Chantal of Greece, *28, princess*
Jeanine Pirro, *45, New York DA*
Brad Pitt, *33, actor*
Kamar de los Reyes, *29, actor*
Rebecca Romijn, *24, model*
Gavin Rossdale, *29, Bush singer*
Winona Ryder, *25, actress*
Paul Sereno, *39, paleontologist*
Spice Girls, *21-24, singers*
Gwen Stefani, *27, lead singer, No Doubt*
Kristin Scott Thomas, *36, actress*
Liv Tyler, *19, actress*
Garrett Wang, *28, actor*
Oprah Winfrey, *43, talk queen*
Michelle Yeoh, *33, actress*

LEONARDO DiCAPRIO, Hollywood's last Romeo, next ventured *Titanic*.

KRISTIN SCOTT THOMAS, of *English (Patient)* birth and fame, lives in Paris.

The Good, the Bad & Oops

Fashion was a field of landmarks and pitfalls

◄ **MIRA SORVINO** proved elegant and poised beyond her 29 years.

◄ Show me the moxie! **CUBA GOODING JR.** is sleek without coming off slick in his Armani suit.

➤ **TONI BRAXTON** likes it hot but still maintains the bearing of a preacher's daughter.

➤ Ruggedly casual, the Force of style is with **HARRISON FORD.**

84

PEOPLE'S BEST- AND WORST-DRESSED CELEBS OF 1997

BEST

Christine Baranski, *45, actress*
Toni Braxton, *29, singer*
George Clooney, *36, actor*
Celine Dion, *28, singer*
Harrison Ford, *55, actor*
Cuba Gooding Jr., *29, actor*
Carolyn Bessette Kennedy, *31, John's wife*
Bette Midler, *51, singer*
Winona Ryder, *25, actress*
Mira Sorvino, *29, actress*

WORST

Paula Abdul, *35, dancer*
Justine Bateman, *31, actress*
Mary J. Blige, *26, singer*
Pat Boone, *63, singer*
Eileen Davidson, *38, actress*
Woody Harrelson, *36, actor*
Andie MacDowell, *39, actress*
Matthew McConaughey, *27, actor*
Lea Thompson, *36, actress*
Donald Trump, *51, developer*

◄ On camera, ANDIE MacDOWELL doesn't chew the scenery, but off she seems to wear it.

◄ PAULA ABDUL displays ample animal charms without getting into the Siegfried and Roy look.

◄ Industrial hemp is his cause, but does WOODY HARRELSON think it's smokin' woven?

◄ Be glad that MARY J. BLIGE's big album was *Share My World* and not *Share My Wardrobe.*

WORST WORST WORST WORST WORST WORST WORST WORST WORST

85

"They were so much in love," said L.A. hairdresser to the stars Laurent. "It's so sad."

FAMILY MATTERS

Altered Plans

Brad Pitt and Gwyneth Paltrow shockingly trash their betrothal

G iven their fame, their incomes and their magnificent cheekbones, Brad Pitt's proposal of marriage to Gwyneth Paltrow held all the promise of a magnificent royal wedding—Hollywood-style. Here, after all, was the silver screen's reigning heartthrob, brought to his knees by one of Generation X's most critically acclaimed actresses. Never mind that the two seemed to have little in common. Glamour Guy, born to a former trucking-company executive and a high school counselor, had been reared on macaroni-and-cheese sermons at a Baptist church in Springfield, Missouri. Glamour Girl, by contrast, was the daughter of producer Bruce Paltrow and actress Blythe Danner and had the artsy gloss of one weaned on tony pool parties in Santa Monica and Broadway theater. Still, both families were on board. "We are thrilled," enthused Bruce Paltrow. "We think it's perfect."

The lovers, eventually, did not. Six months after the Big Announcement came another: Pitt, 33, and Paltrow, 24, were ending their 2½-year romance. While the couple refused to field questions, letting their publicists do the talking, a source close to both said, "It's a real relationship with real problems. This is not about any third party." Even in a town where love is as unpredictable as opening-day grosses, the revelation came as a shock. No other celebrity couple in recent years had seemed so like "a happy Romeo and Juliet," as one friend put it.

Pitt seemed to rebound more quickly. Just four days before news of the break-up became public, he was spotted carousing solo at a party. "Brad actually looked really happy, smiling and enjoying himself," says one guest. Paltrow hid out with friends, who held their tongues while Pitt's friends put out their spin. "Brad called it off," said one. "He got caught up in the frenzy of getting married, but he really didn't want to." Another surmised, "He's commitment-shy." Pitt and Paltrow had fallen in love on the set of the murder thriller *Seven*, and the buzz was that they'd costar, as scheduled, in the karaoke-bar road musical *Duets,* directed by her dad. But as the 1998 filming neared, she stayed, he split.

The Split Parade of '97

Seinfeld, Fawcett and two Trumps led the list

◄ After 17 turbulent years (and one son, Redmond, 12), Hollywood's most celebrated never-marrieds, Farrah Fawcett, 50, and Ryan O'Neal, 56, said adios. No third party was to blame. "As chaotic and crazy as their relationship was," said photographer Davis Factor, who shot her for *Playboy* in 1995, "I don't know who could put up with the two of them better than each other."

She liked to party with rappers in Manhattan; he enjoyed nesting in their $10 million suburban mansion. Four years after marrying her mentor, pop princess Mariah Carey, 28, began to feel trapped. In May, Carey and Tommy Mottola, 47, the Sony Music chief, announced their separation.

▲ Just shy of their seventh anniversary, speed skater Dan Jansen, 31, filed for divorce from Robin, 38, who had stuck by through years of disappointments before his dramatic gold medal in 1994. Reports linked Dan with another woman; Robin insisted she wanted to reconcile.

➤ Screen siren Geena Davis, 41, and director Renny Harlin, 39, called a halt to their marriage after nearly four years. When they were later spotted arguing good-naturedly over who should buy popcorn at a flick, the word was that Davis wanted to stay pals—but was fed up with Harlin's wandering eye.

Having sired 13 children by two wives and three mistresses, actor Anthony Quinn, 82, began to put his life in order, finally divorcing his wife of 20 years, Iolanda, 62. After devastating court testimony in which their middle son Danny (below right, with mom and brother Francesco) accused him of beating her—Quinn forked over about half of his reported $15 million estate. Then, belatedly in December, he wed Kathy Benvin, 35 (with him in the limo), mother of his last two kids.

◄ Billy Bob Thornton, 41, may be on a roll as director, writer and actor, but when it came to marriage, he just couldn't get it right. In April, fourth wife Pietra Dawn Thornton, 27, filed for divorce, then in June obtained a restraining order against Thornton, claiming he "has hit me, punched me, bit me . . . sometimes in front of [our two] children."

▼ There's no question that Madonna, 38, is keeping her baby, but Papa is out of the romantic picture—if not the family album. Aspiring actor and part-time personal trainer Carlos Leon, 31, moved out of Madonna's mansion in May. But he continues to visit regularly the couple's daughter, Lourdes, who turned 1 in October.

▼ When Jeff Goldblum, 44, was saying, "I am single right now," wife Laura Dern, 30, insisted, "Jeff is going to be in my life forever." Then rumors linked her with Billy Bob Thornton, and Dern denied any romance. But by June, she and Thornton (unlike she and Goldblum) seemed to be a recurring item.

◄ They became dumbstruck by each other on the set of *Dumb & Dumber*. But just 10 months after tying the knot, Jim Carrey, 35, and Lauren Holly, 31, filed for divorce. An insider reported that she may have tired of living in her hubby's frantic, antic shadow: "She wanted to prove she could go out on her own."

▼ Four years after they met in Central Park in 1993, Jerry Seinfeld, 43, and Shoshanna Lonstein, 22, went bust. But on-again rumors persisted until October when Lonstein's new beau, Jay Aston, 23, said that he and she were planning to wed and open a health spa.

▲ After their 14-year union broke up, Kirstie Alley, 46, got custody of their two kids and a new sitcom. Parker Stevenson, 45, got divorce proceedings moved to the communal property state of California.

Oh, those wacky, luckless wives of Donald Trump. Seven years ago, Ivana made spectator sport of her sagging 13-year marriage by shouting at The Donald's then-mistress Marla, "You bitch, leave my husband alone!" Four years later, Marla (left) grabbed headlines when, after birthing Donald's child, she and Trump wed. In May, Marla, 33, and Donald, 50, called it quits—conveniently for him months shy of a milestone in their prenuptial agreement that would have boosted her divorce settlement considerably. Weeks later, Ivana (right), 48, split with multimillionaire Riccardo Mazzucchelli, 54, after just 20 months of marriage.

▼ Robert James Waller, 58, the pop laureate of midlife lust (*The Bridges of Madison County*) took up with the 34-year-old yard woman on his Texas ranch and divorced his wife of 36 years, Georgia, 56 (right).

◄ April 12 should have been a day of celebration: It was country singer Vince Gill's 40th birthday, and the 17th anniversary of his marriage to singer Janis Gill, 43. Instead, Janis failed to show for a performance with her husband in Nashville. Four days later, she filed for divorce.

▼ Director *(Boyz N the Hood)* John Singleton, 29, citing irreconcilable differences, filed for divorce in April from his wife, Akosua Busia, 30. The couple, who wed in October 1996, have a baby daughter, Hadar.

➤ For Neve Campbell, 23, there was success on the set of *Party of Five*—and jealousy from Jeff Colt, 33, an aspiring actor, at home. Shortly after their second anniversary, the pair separated.

His Game, Her Set—a Match

After a three-year courtship, Brooke Shields weds her ace of hearts, Andre Agassi

Like so many brides on their big day, Brooke Shields awoke on April 19 determined to steer clear of her fiancé until the evening ceremony that would plight her troth to tennis star Andre Agassi. When the actress, a Princeton alum who plays a sweet klutz on NBC's *Suddenly Susan*, still felt jittery after an hour-long massage, she went for a stroll. Finding a soft patch of grass, she lay down and began to meditate—until the hotel's sprinkler system went off. Unfazed, the famously good-natured star wrote it off as a "*Suddenly Susan* moment," and continued preparing for her nuptials.

At 6:15 p.m., Agassi, 26, decked out not in grunge but a classic Alfred Dunhill tuxedo, arrived at St. John's Episcopal Chapel in Monterey, California. Thirty minutes later, as a nine-piece string and wind ensemble played "Gabriel's Oboe," Shields, 31, carrying a lily-of-the-valley bouquet, entered the candlelit chapel packed with white roses, calla lilies and 150 guests, including *Susan* costar Judd Nelson and Nastassja Kinski. As her maid of honor, two bridesmaids and her mother (and ex-manager), Teri, preceded her down the aisle, Shields glowed in a corseted ivory Heidi Weisel gown with a pleated skirt and a 16-foot-long antique lace veil. "I've never seen a sparkle in Andre's eyes like when he looked at her," says Andre's brother Phillip, 34, one of the two groomsmen. After the exchange of vows, the newlyweds rode off in a horse-drawn carriage to a resort in Carmel Valley, where celebrants danced until well past midnight. "It was so romantic," observed guest Edwige Fareed. "If perfection exists, this was it."

Robin's Nesting Instinct

Batman sidekick Chris O'Donnell ties the knot

Just moments before the April 19 ceremony at St. Patrick's Church in downtown Washington, D.C., was set to begin, the pint-size ring bearer burst into tears and refused to go on. While 250 guests waited in the rose- and lily-filled chapel, the groom, *Batman Forever* star Chris O'Donnell, 26, transformed into Super Uncle, engaging nephew Matthew Murphy in a mini man-to-man chat. Then the tyke proceeded down the aisle, lead- ing the procession that heralded the arrival of the bride, Caroline Fentress, 24, a kindergarten teacher and O'Donnell's longtime girlfriend. After the hour-long cer- emony, which involved a full Catholic mass, the newly- weds enjoyed their first dance to Jerome Kern's "The Way You Look Tonight." Soon, the party was pumping as O'Donnell and old pals from his hometown of Chicago and from his Boston College days led the room in the conga line, and in the requisite hooting to the Isley Brothers' "Shout." Boy Wonder and bride did not run out of steam until almost 2 a.m. Little Matthew's melt- down apart, "It was a wonderful wedding," says Fen- tress's mother Diane. "Perfect from beginning to end."

And the Bells Kept Ringing

Kelsey, Kenny, Scottie, Duchovny . . . they all did the right thing

▲ The sun was setting and the bride's diamond-and-topaz earrings (a gift from the groom) were sparkling as *Frasier* star Kelsey Grammer, 42, wed *Playboy* model Camille Donatacci, 28, on a rented 1,000-acre Malibu ranch. Donatacci became the third Mrs. Grammer 11 months after the actor was treated at the Betty Ford Center for a drinking problem.

◄ A year and a half after actor Robert De Niro, 53, gave former flight attendant Grace Hightower, 42, a reported 10-carat emerald-cut diamond ring, the two cemented their on-again, off-again romance in a private ceremony in upstate New York. Among the 11-member wedding party: bestfellas Harvey Keitel and Joe Pesci.

➤ First came love in 1989. Next came baby Sophia in 1996. In 1997 at last came marriage for Sylvester Stallone, 50, and model Jennifer Flavin, 28. The two have been through a lot. In 1994, Stallone dumped Flavin via Federal Express. Last year, they held fast as a family as infant Sophia had heart surgery.

▼ With four marriages behind him, Kenny Rogers, 58, was in no rush this time. Though Wanda Miller, 30, caught his eye instantly when he entered the Atlanta restaurant where she was then a hostess, it would be four more years before he literally serenaded her at the altar. *The Gambler* knows when to hold 'em.

▼ For once, Chicago Bull Scottie Pippen, 31, didn't have to dodge Michael Jordan's long shadow when he exchanged July vows with student Larsa Younan, 23, in the Windy City. It was the all-star forward's second trip to the altar, Younan's first.

◄ It was the ultimate power wedding when Supreme Court Associate Justice Ruth Bader Ginsburg presided over the April nuptials of Federal Reserve Chairman Alan Greenspan, 71, and his love of 12 years, NBC's chief foreign-affairs correspondent Andrea Mitchell, 50. The flower girl was Mitchell's goddaughter Lauren Hunt.

▼ Their four-month courtship had been as furtive as an *X-Files* conspiracy. So was their wedding. With just six guests in attendance, *X-Files* hunk David Duchovny, 36, wed Téa Leoni, 31, lanky star of NBC's *The Naked Truth*.

▼ It was a feast for sore eyes when Ken Wahl, 40, star of the old CBS series *Wiseguy*, wed *Playboy* centerfold Shane Barbi, 41, outside Las Vegas at Lake Mead. Both the bride and groom were married once before.

◄ The Peter Duchin orchestra played until 2 a.m. after Matthew Broderick, 35, and Sarah Jessica Parker, 32, sanctified their five-year relationship. The Episcopal ceremony was performed by the actor's sister, the Reverend Janet Broderick Kraft.

► Christopher Darden, 41, who became a household name when he prosecuted O.J. Simpson, wed Marcia Carter, a TV executive, in August. It is a first marriage for both. Darden, however, has an infant daughter from a previous relationship, and is seeking custody.

◄ Scottish model Kirsty Hume, 21, got to the Loch Lomond church 30 minutes past time. But singer Donovan Leitch, 29, didn't get itchy in his skivvyless kilts. His dad, '60s rocker Donovan, who healed a 20-year rift with his son, said he was "proud."

99

During her marathon labor, Locklear got two roses and a foot-long sub sandwich from jokester Sambora. Heather and her sister take Ava for a checkup.

That's One Sexy Mama!

Melrose Place vixen Heather Locklear joins the new moms' club

Her pregnancy had been as problem-free as her series, *Melrose Place*, had been crisis-plagued. But by 11:30 p.m. on October 3, having logged 35 hours of labor, Heather Locklear was wearing down—and the baby was resisting delivery. Finally, the doctor suggested performing a C-section. After a reassuring hug from her husband, Bon Jovi guitarist Richie Sambora, 38, she said simply, "Let's go." Thirty-five minutes later, Ava Elizabeth Sambora made her debut. "Heather," says her own mother Diane, "will make a great mom." Locklear, 36, has had babies on her mind since as far back as 1992 when her marriage to first husband Mötley Crüe drummer Tommy Lee dissolved. Asked if she wanted to marry again, Locklear answered "I absolutely do, because I want children." Motherhood, however, is not a concept fans equate with either her sexy, conniving *Melrose* character or Locklear herself, who has become the American male teenager's favorite libidinous fixation. So cameramen shot around Locklear's pregnancy last season. And Locklear, who took daily walks and pumped light weights throughout the gestation and then took care of Ava without help, should be back to eye-popping, size-2 form by her return to the set.

Pop-Star Papa

Michael Jackson revels in his new son, and can't resist sharing the joy with the cameras

It's not every kid who has his own backyard merry-go-round. But then it's not every kid who has Elizabeth Taylor and Macaulay Culkin for godparents. And it's not every kid whose father moon-walked his way to millions without ever setting foot on the moon. Born February 13, Prince Michael Joseph Jackson Jr. is the crown jewel in Michael Jackson's sprawling empire. "I'm in bliss 24 hours a day," Jackson allowed in a rare interview, before ducking behind the gates of Neverland, his California estate, with appeals to allow the boy his privacy. "I grew up in a fishbowl," Jackson said, "and I will not allow that to happen to my child."

Since then, Jackson, 38, seems to have changed his mind. In March he sold photos of the baby—named Prince after Jackson's grandfather and great-grandfather—for a reported $2 million to Britain's OK! magazine. While the funds were earmarked for Jackson's Heal the World children's foundation, the deal was—like just about everything else in his life—questioned. By selling access, wrote columnist Liz Smith, he "hasn't convinced anybody of his sincere desire to have the child 'lead a normal life.' " Jackson posed again with the boy for the December LIFE, this time noting, "When he first came out, he had my grandfather's and brothers' and La Toya's shape of head. He has Debbie's chin." Debbie, of course, is Debbie Rowe, 37, the dermatologist's assistant whom Jackson wed three months before Prince was born and who still lives 150 miles southeast in Van Nuys. But the infatuated dad has two nurses on call and frequent visits from his ex, Lisa Marie Presley, while Debbie carries their second child, a daughter to be named Paris Michael Catherine.

Look Who's Nesting

Now on diaper duty: Melissa Etheridge and, would you believe, Tony Randall?

◄ *Seinfeld* fixture Julia Louis-Dreyfus, 36, and her husband, Brad Hall, 39, an actor, writer and TV producer, welcomed 7-lb. 8-oz. Charles in Los Angeles. The couple also has a 5-year-old son, Henry.

► Mum(s) was the word after filmmaker Julie Cypher, 32 (right), companion of rocker Melissa Etheridge, 35, gave birth to Bailey Jean Cypher. The couple declined to say how the girl was conceived.

◄ *Baywatch* babe Gena Lee Nolin, 25, and husband Greg Fahlman, 37, a video producer, became first-time parents to a son, Spencer Michael.

► Country crooners Faith Hill, 29, and husband Tim McGraw, 29, greeted their first child, daughter Gracie Katherine, in—where else?—Nashville.

Actor Tony Randall, 77, finally became a father when his wife, Heather Harlan, 27, gave birth on April 11 to a girl. They are expecting a second child next June. A disciplinarian, Randall says he will raise them on classical music and no TV.

▼ Actor Pierce Brosnan, 44, and his lady friend, *Unsolved Mysteries* correspondent Keely Schaye Smith, 33, welcomed a 9-lb. boy, Dylan Thomas. Brosnan has two adult stepchildren and a teenage son from his marriage to the late actress Cassandra Harris.

▲ In New York City, balladeer Harry Connick Jr., 30, and his wife, model Jill Goodacre, 33, were delighted by the September arrival of 7-lb. 4-oz. daughter Sara Kate. The couple also has a 1-year-old daughter, Georgia.

What Kept You?

A fragile preemie lives to greet his twin brother, born 92 days later

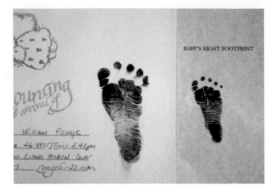

At birth, Jacob's foot dwarfed Joshua's; below, Janet pacifies newbie Jacob, while Ray holds big bro.

Janet Pasaye was back in her hospital room at the Columbia Hoffman Estates Medical Center in suburban Chicago, after watching the Super Bowl on January 26 with her husband, Ray, when she saw her newborn for the first time. Delivered by cesarean section six hours earlier, Jacob had weighed in at 6 lbs. 1 oz. But to Pasaye he looked like a football lineman. "I was like, 'Oh, my God, he's so big,'" she says. "I was used to Joshua."

Joshua had been born prematurely in October, 92 days earlier. Yet, incredibly, he is Jacob's twin. (The previous record span between the birth of one twin and another was 36 days.) Delivered at about 25 weeks, Joshua weighed just 1 lb. 5 oz. and was so fragile that his parents weren't permitted to hold him. Thanks to a procedure known as delayed-interval delivery, Jacob was given more time in the uterus and a better chance to live. "I didn't want two babies struggling for life," recalls Pasaye, 35.

For a full month and a half, Pasaye, a project manager at a Chicago print brokerage firm, lay in bed. On January 25 she stopped taking her labor-suppressing medication, and hours later contractions began. Pasaye brought Jacob home three days later, and Joshua left the hospital a few weeks after that, weighing nearly 5 lbs. Despite his difficult debut, Pasaye doubts anyone will push him around. "I envision Joshua being a big rugged guy that's going to protect his younger brother," she says. "He's a fighter."

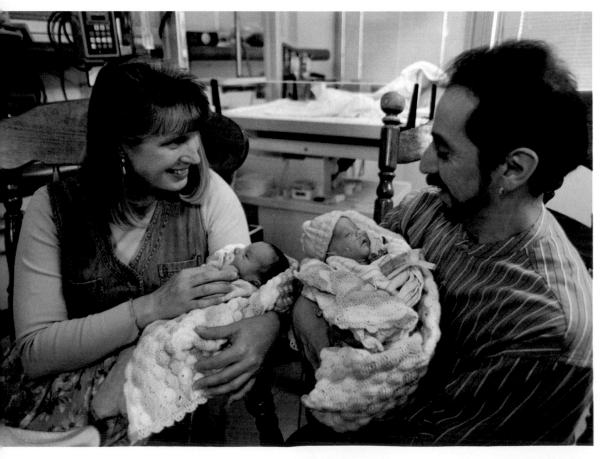

Seeing Double at 51

Actress Adrienne Barbeau beats the odds

The chances of conceiving after age 50 are less than 1 percent, though that number increases by as much as 40 percent if a woman uses a donor egg. Adrienne Barbeau, 51, won't say exactly which fertility method worked for her and her husband, TV writer-producer Billy Van Zandt, 39. But the outcome is a stunner. On March 17, the star of the 1970s sitcom *Maude* gave birth to identical twin sons, Walker and William. And catch this: Barbeau did it naturally, without the use of painkillers.

Even before they wed in 1992, Barbeau and Van Zandt talked about having a child of their own. (Barbeau shares custody of her son Cody, 12, with her ex, horror-film director John Carpenter.) "Family has always been the most important thing to me," says Van Zandt. But when nothing happened for four years, he began to reconcile himself to the likelihood they would not have children. Then, the miracle happened. After the twins' birth, the new father took naturally to fretting about his sons' well-being. "The first day I left [for the office]," he says, "I felt like a deadbeat dad." Barbeau is adjusting her own way. "I do have a lot of energy now," she says. "And being older, I'm calmer and more relaxed." Of course, compared to some, Barbeau is a spring chicken. Californian Arceli Keh beat Barbeau to the delivery room by months—and years—becoming a mom at 63.

1978

1979

1988

They may wear spats, but they swear they never have them. Donald, who co-owns a firm that makes plastic pink flamingos, says, "We've never had a disagreement."

Birds of a Featherstone

Yup. Matching outfits, every day, for 17 years—and counting

It's morning in Fitchburg, Massachusetts, and Donald and Nancy Featherstone are venturing forth to meet the world, looking just like two peas in a pod—if peas ever appeared in tiger stripes. Tiger stripes—on Donald's shirt and Nancy's dress—just happen to be the motif du jour. Tomorrow, it could be a loud Hawaiian print, his-and-her Chesterfield coats with bowler hats, or something Disney-themed. Whatever the look, they will be dressed alike, as they have been every day for the last 17 years. Though the Featherstones married in 1976, one year after meeting at a hardware convention, they didn't adopt the me-too style until around 1980. As Nancy, who designs and sews the duo's garments, explains, "It's a way of staying connected."

Aloha from Maui
1991

1993

1996

Forever and a Day

America's longest-married couple celebrates Year 81

Newspapers cost a penny and Woodrow Wilson was President the year George Couron first laid eyes on Gaynel Emery. Smitten while passing her on a sidewalk in Fort Dodge, Iowa, he fell in love when they met again at a carnival. He was 18, she was sweet 16,

and after their marriage a year later in 1916, they dreamed of a long life. "As far as age," says George, "we thought we might get up to 80." They did—two decades ago. Now George, 100, and Ganyel, 97, have crossed another threshold to celebrate their 81st anniversary in their current home of Orangevale, California, making them the longest-married living couple in the U.S. (Two other couples, both now deceased, share the record of 86 years.) The Courons' blissful union has produced 14 children, 43 grandchildren, 72 great-grand-children and some 30 great-greats. Gaynel, who is now blind and frail, says, "I got the man I wanted." George, not to be outdone, choruses, "And I got the woman I wanted." Then he gazes at his bride and sighs, "What a beautiful woman this is."

James Stewart

He was everything his screen persona suggested: easygoing yet savvy, ordinary yet heroic

In 75 feature films, James Stewart took his place in the first rank of leading men of Hollywood's golden age. With the classic *It's a Wonderful Life,* he became a staple of America's holiday season. Yet onscreen and off, Stewart appeared to be utterly unassuming, a genial man with an unhurried manner who could make being ordinary seem the most appealing thing in the world. "There was no star quality about him," says Ernest Borgnine, his costar in *Flight of the Phoenix.* "He was Jimmy Stewart. Period." When Stewart died at 89 from failing health and heart problems, some of the music of midcentury America died with him.

Lanky and handsome, Stewart was the datingest bachelor in Hollywood in the 1930s and 1940s, squiring the likes of Loretta Young, Ginger Rogers, Marlene Dietrich and Olivia de Havilland. He was a shrewd businessman, too, in the 1950s becoming one of Hollywood's first free agents. By negotiating

From his 1936 studio still (opposite page) to his signature work, *It's a Wonderful Life* (above), Stewart was forever. So was his marriage to Gloria (right).

contracts that often gave him what was then unusual—a percentage of box office receipts in lieu of a salary—he became one of his generation's richest stars. Yet his life was low-key and unscandalous. Though it took Stewart until the age of 41 to marry, once he settled down he settled deep, remaining devoted to his wife, Gloria, through 45 years of a marriage that produced twin daughters, an overflowing vegetable patch and a house full of cats and dogs.

All his life, Stewart admitted to a passive streak in his nature. "I don't act," he once said. "I react." Part of his legend insists that he didn't so much climb to the top as float there. His upward drift started in the small town of Indiana, Pennsylvania, where his father ran a prosperous family hardware store founded in 1853. In 1932, as he was graduating from Princeton with a degree in architecture, Jimmy was invited to join a small repertory company on Cape Cod. He thought summer stock might be a nice way to meet girls. When the troupe was offered a New York City showcase, Stewart went along in a bit part. The play was a flop, but good reviews in his next few roles brought him a $350-a-week contract with MGM. Stewart got his best roles when he was lent to other studios. At Columbia, director Frank Capra cast him in two films, the second of which, 1939's *Mr. Smith Goes to Washington,* made him a star. A year later, Stewart's performance in *The Philadelphia Story* brought him the Academy Award for Best Actor.

Instead of cashing in as the war approached, he enlisted in the Army Air Corps. Eventually he flew more than 20 missions, returning home with a Distinguished Flying Cross and winding up a brigadier general in the Reserve. His first postwar project, *It's a Wonderful Life,* won Stewart his third Oscar nomination. After several flops, *Harvey, Rear Window* and *Anatomy of a Murder* reenergized his career, which continued until 1978. He once proposed his own epitaph: "He gave people a lot of pleasure." Such modesty might have seemed disingenuous coming from any other Hollywood legend; coming from Stewart, it charmed and rang true.

John Denver

Life's troubles couldn't dim a singer's natural sunniness

For a man whose music extolled nature's serenity, John Denver's violent, watery death when his two-seat airplane nose-dived into California's Monterey Bay seemed an anomaly. But so, in a way, had his career. In the 1970s, a decade bloated with the flamboyance and musi-cal excesses of the likes of David Bowie and Kiss, the homespun troubadour's melodic songs ("Rocky Mountain High," "Sunshine on My Shoulders") and crys-talline voice struck a refreshing chord. "He was the Jimmy Stewart of folk mu-sic," says Mary Travers, of Peter, Paul & Mary. Certainly, Denver's appeal was broad. He earned no fewer than four platinum and 12 gold albums in the U.S. alone. His infectious enthusiasm crossed over first to television, where he hosted some 20 specials, then to film, where he starred with George Burns in the 1977 comedy *Oh, God!*

The son of a hard-drinking Air Force test pilot, Denver, 53, grew up with a passion for airplanes. With royalties from his 1974 hit album *Back Home Again,* Denver bought a Learjet—which he piloted himself to concerts after his dad taught him how to fly in 1976. Two days after Denver's crash, officials an-nounced that he had been flying with-out the medical certificate necessary for all approved pilots. It had reported-ly been suspended because Denver had twice been arrested on drunk-driving charges, one of those times totaling his Porsche on his way home in Aspen.

His personal life, too, had hidden edges. On the 15th anniversary of his first marriage, his wife, Annie (for whom he wrote his 1974 hit "Annie's Song" and with whom he adopted two children), asked for a divorce. His second marriage ended in divorce following rumors of infidelity, a problem that had also plagued his first marriage. But before his death, he and his second wife were close again, bound together by devotion to their 8-year-old daughter.

Brandon Tartikoff

With *Cheers, Miami Vice* and other hits, NBC's televisionary changed the face of prime time

After Brandon Tartikoff suggested during a Yale fiction writing seminar how to jazz up the plot of a D.H. Lawrence short story, the professor, author Robert Penn Warren, said, "Young man, have you ever considered a career in television?" Advice has seldom been sounder. In 1980, at age 31, Tartikoff became the youngest person ever put in charge of network programming. He proceeded not only to take NBC from worst to first in the Nielsen ratings but also to change the TV landscape with such blockbusters as *The Cosby Show* and *St. Elsewhere.* While his career surged only upward, life was not as kind. Tartikoff battled Hodgkin's disease for two decades prior to his death at 48. In 1991 he made a left-hand turn into an oncoming car, a mistake that left his 8-year-old daughter in a coma for six weeks. (In 1994, Tartikoff and his wife of 15 years adopted a second daughter.) He once explained his recipe for success: "I don't give the public what they want. I'm more interested in giving them what they will want."

Red Skelton

Despite grievous personal losses, TV's redheaded clown prince made laughter and delight his life's work

With a hit squad of alter egos—Mean Widdle Kid, Clem Kadiddlehopper and Freddie the Freeloader—Red Skelton was the clown prince of TV from 1951 to 1971. "Some of today's comics have witty repartee, others are good in sketches, some are physical, and some never speak," says Steve Allen, a friend of Skelton's until his death of pneumonia at 84. "But Red could do all of the above. He was a natural clown." Skelton's father was a circus clown who died two months before the birth of Richard Bernard—the youngest of four boys. Left destitute, Skelton's mother scraped by as a cleaning woman. At 14, Red, as his brother nicknamed him, dropped out of school to sing "mammy" songs in blackface with a traveling minstrel show, then turned to burlesque. At age 19 he married Edna Marie Stillwell, an usher who soon began managing his career. After Skelton's big break in 1937 on Rudy Vallee's radio show, Stillwell negotiated a movie contract that led to some 40 films in 13 years. Although they divorced during those years, she continued as his manager.

By the time his long-running *Red Skelton Hour* premiered on CBS in 1953, Skelton had remarried and was the father of two children. In 1958 son Richard, 9, died of leukemia. "The death of his child did Red in," says actress Arlene Dahl. Skelton and his second wife, Georgia, divorced in 1973, the same year Skelton married for a third time. Three years later, Georgia committed suicide.

By then CBS had cancelled Skelton's highly rated show, deeming it too unhip. "My heart was broken," Skelton admitted. But he returned to the stage until he was well into his 70s. Long enough to affect a new generation of comics, including Jim Carrey and *Seinfeld*'s Michael Richards, who in 1993 inducted his boyhood idol into the Comedy Hall of Fame.

Pat Paulsen

Campaigning for President was his primary shtick

It was 1996. Bob Dole was running for President. So was Pat Paulsen. Again. Dole floated an idea he thought would put him in the White House—slash federal taxes 15 percent. Paulsen had his own notion. "I think we should just tip the government if it does a good job," he said. "Fifteen percent is the standard tip, isn't it?" For almost 30 years, Paulsen had a Pat solution to the nation's problems—or at least a memorable comment. When the dour-faced comic died at age 69 in Mexico, where he was undergoing alternative therapy for colon and brain cancer, he took an election-year institution with him. Paulsen's political career—he ran for President five times—began in 1968 at the urging of Tom and Dick Smothers, on whose show he appeared. "Why not?" he responded. "I can't dance." His first time out he got some 200,000 votes. After the *Smothers Brothers Comedy Hour* was sacked by CBS, Paulsen briefly headlined his own show on ABC, then opened a winery that he sold in 1992. Diagnosed with cancer three years later he continued to perform with the support of his fourth wife, Noma. Three weeks before Paulsen died, ex-President Gerald Ford phoned, says Noma, "to say how much more he enjoyed Pat's campaigns than his own."

Mother Teresa

The Saint of Calcutta's streets made her life a gift to the world

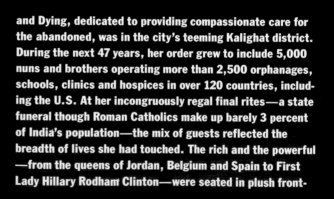

The reach of her influence seemed never to change her. Until illness in 1996 forced Mother Teresa to modify her daily routine, she rose at 4:30 each morning and kept to a frugal diet of rice and vegetables. All the donations and monetary awards that came her way—including the more than $190,000 that accompanied her 1979 Nobel Peace Prize—went to fund new orphanages, hospices and homes for those suffering from leprosy. After Mother Teresa died of cardiac arrest at 87 at the Calcutta base of the Missionaries of Charity, the Roman Catholic order she founded in 1950, thousands of mourners—rich and poor, Hindu, Muslim and Christian—braved monsoon rains to pay their respects to the woman whom they affectionately called the "saint of the gutters." Echoing sentiments voiced round the world, President Clinton declared, "The world has lost one of the giants of our time. She led by serving and showed us the stunning power of simple humility."

Such impact probably would have been unimaginable to young Agnes Gonxha Bojaxhiu, one of three children born to an Albanian couple in Macedonia. After her father, a prosperous building contractor, died when Agnes was around 7, her devout family was reduced to genteel poverty. At 12, Agnes felt a calling to help the poor; at 18 she joined a community of Irish nuns known for their missionary work and took the

name of the 19th-century French nun St. Thérèse of Lisieux. After training in Dublin and Darjeeling, India, the new Sister Teresa taught upper-class Bengali girls at St. Mary's High School in Calcutta and eventually became the school's principal.

At the age of 36, while on a train from Calcutta to Darjeeling, she received what she took to be a divine message. "I was to give up all," she wrote in her 1995 book *A Simple Path,* "and follow Jesus into the slums."

It would take another two years to persuade the Vatican to let her leave the cloister, live among the poor and begin her work in Calcutta's streets. Her first Home for the Destitute and Dying, dedicated to providing compassionate care for the abandoned, was in the city's teeming Kalighat district. During the next 47 years, her order grew to include 5,000 nuns and brothers operating more than 2,500 orphanages, schools, clinics and hospices in over 120 countries, including the U.S. At her incongruously regal final rites—a state funeral though Roman Catholics make up barely 3 percent of India's population—the mix of guests reflected the breadth of lives she had touched. The rich and the powerful—from the queens of Jordan, Belgium and Spain to First Lady Hillary Rodham Clinton—were seated in plush front-

row chairs, while representatives of the afflicted, whom Mother Teresa cherished—a leper, a deaf man and an ex-prisoner—were ushered in to offer symbolic gifts of wine, bread and water. Her small white coffin arrived on the World War II-era gun carriage that had borne Mahatma Gandhi, the father of Indian independence, to his funeral pyre.

Though hailed as a saint, Mother Teresa was not without her detractors. British journalist Christopher Hitchens, in his 1994 TV documentary *Hell's Angel* and his 1995 *Missionary Position,* savaged her for appealing for clemency on behalf of Charles Keating—the infamous central figure in the U.S. savings-and-loan scandal—after accepting $1.25 million in donations from him. Yet the feisty nun, who once kept Princess Diana waiting for an audience (the two met for the last time in New York City in June 1997, opposite page) and made a visiting U.S. journalist put in a day's work in the Calcutta hospice before granting an interview, forgave Hitchens. "What one has to understand about Mother Teresa is that she sees Christ in every person she encounters," says biographer Kathryn Spink. "I have heard her say that every human being must be given the opportunity to do good." Certainly, when her own opportunity came, she made the most of it.

Robert Mitchum

Whether busting heads or breaking hearts, Hollywood's bad boy kept working, stayed married and defined noir

Charisma? Not exactly. Talent? Without a doubt. But what really set Robert Mitchum apart from the big screen's other tough guys was his mystique, which projected both violence and sensuality, yet never failed to charm. Though he was one of Hollywood's more venerated stars, Mitchum never took himself or the movie business too seriously. "Training to be an actor is like going to school to learn to be tall," he once said.

Though notorious for his hard drinking, public brawls and an infamous pot bust back in 1948, Mitchum continued to make films right up to his death at 79 from emphysema and lung cancer. Perhaps more notable, for Hollywood at any rate, the hunky sex symbol managed to stay married to the same woman for 57 years, despite two brief separations and rumors of dalliances with such leading ladies as Jane Russell and Shirley MacLaine.

Born in Connecticut, Mitchum was raised by various relatives, ran away often and worked during the Depression as a coal miner, prizefighter and jazz saxophonist. Settling in California in the 1930s, he eventually took a job as a stagehand and drifted into acting, starting out playing heavies in Hopalong Cassidy movies. He went on to appear in more than 100 films, many of them turkeys churned out by RKO. But somehow Mitchum always seemed to shine through the dreary material. He received his only Oscar nomination for the heroic Lieutenant Walker in the 1945 film *The Story of G. I. Joe.* But his defining roles were in the moody classics *Crossfire* and *Out of the Past,* and in his eerie portrayal of murderous psychopaths in *The Night of the Hunter* and *Cape Fear.* "You could even say," says director Martin Scorsese, "that Mitchum *was* film noir."

Colonel Tom Parker

He made Elvis millions—and pocketed a few himself

Though Colonel Tom Parker flaunted his flamboyantly bad taste in clothes, he worked overtime to shroud his past. It is believed that he was born in Holland and entered the U.S. while working as a barker with a traveling carnival. This much is certain: In 1955, while promoting country-music acts, he met Elvis Presley. Parker—by then dubbed the Colonel—swiftly engineered three starmaking TV appearances on *The Ed Sullivan Show,* and soon the pair was Hollywood bound. As Presley's lifelong manager, Parker designed contracts that steered up to half the star's multimillions into his own pockets. In 1981, four years after Presley's death, Parker was charged with enriching himself at the singer's expense; a Memphis court then stripped him of any legal rights to the Presley estate. Even so, the twice-married Parker, who died at 87 from stroke complications, will be remembered as a dazzling dealmaker. Says Beecher Smith II, one of Presley's Memphis lawyers: "He was a showman and promoter right up there with P.T. Barnum."

Roy Lichtenstein

From his brush came a charming, sardonic
oeuvre for the books—and not just the comics

It might be argued that his was the antithesis of art: boldly derivative, baldly impersonal, at times provocatively
bad. In 1964, LIFE magazine went so far as to ask, "Is he
the worst artist in America?" But Roy Lichtenstein, who
died at 73 of complications resulting from pneumonia, was
one artist of the Pop school who knew precisely what he
was about. As he lifted images from the popular culture—
ranging from bubble-gum wrappers and comics to master-
works by Picasso—and re-created them in ironic paintings, murals, prints and sculptures, he managed to tweak
highbrows, pay homage to lowbrows, and never stray from
his subversive vision. Born in New York City, Lichtenstein
turned his full attention to art after Army service during
World War II. His breakthrough show came in 1962, estab-
lishing him as the renegade who painted comics, a reputation that would endure, although his cartoon period ended
by the mid-1960s. (So did the first of his two marriages.)
"He lived for his work . . . never making inflated claims for
it, never posing as a maestro," eulogized critic Robert
Hughes. "The humor of his art came from a natural sweet-
ness of temperament."

Willem de Kooning

A fleeing Dutchman became America's
great master of Abstract Expressionism

His was the sort of work that announced its author without
need of signature. Whether the canvas depicted a woman or
a landscape, the splash of color and emotion were
pure Willem de Kooning. "His brush stroke," says
critic Mark Stevens, "is one of the most distinctive in the history of art, immediately recogniz-
able, full of verve and poetry." And his effect?
"There was something rough and ready about his
painting that was particularly American." De
Kooning, however, was not American—at least
not during his formative years. Born in Holland to
a barmaid, he did not reach the land of his infatu-
ation until he was 22, jumping ship in Hoboken,

Woman (Green)

New Jersey. He supported himself as a house painter and
commercial artist until his first one-man show in 1948. Then
his *Woman* series of the 1950s, a group of bright, violent
paintings loosely based on the female form, established him
as a giant of Abstract Expressionism. *Interchange,* a 1955
cityscape, was auctioned for $20.6 million in 1989, a record
then and now for a contemporary artist.

Head-turningly handsome, with charm to match, de Kooning had a reputation for heavy drinking and turbulent rela-
tionships with women. In his later years the
woman he battled most was his daughter Lisa,
who tried to exert greater control over his life after he began to suffer from Alzheimer's disease,
which eventually killed him at 92. In 1989 a court
declared de Kooning mentally incompetent.
Though there has been speculation that after
the disease's onset his studio assistants collaborated in his output, de Kooning's six decades
of prodigious production ensure his reputation
as one of his adopted land's great masters.

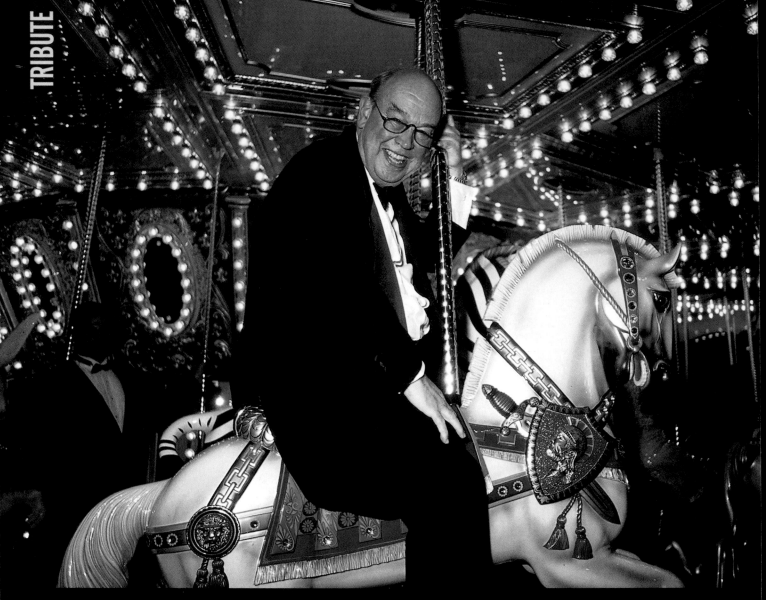

Charles Kuralt

With fond wit and a sense of poetry,
he caught the heartbeat of America

Even as a 20-year-old rookie reporter on North Carolina's *Charlotte News,* Charles Kuralt had his own unique slant on assignments. Sent to cover a parade, he focused on one of the pint-size spectators—a little boy watching through a thicket of grown-up legs. Kuralt, it seems, decided to "get down on his knees," remembers Richard Cole, dean of the University of North Carolina journalism school, "and write about how the parade appeared to that young kid." A genial populist who never lost his sense of wonder, Kuralt spent most of his 42-year career at CBS celebrating small amaze-

ments that others overlooked. By the time he died of heart failure at 62, he himself was celebrated as a broadcast institution, heralded for his warmth and the unexcelled grace of his work. "There was a humility in his demeanor," says Charles Osgood, his successor on the estimable *CBS Sunday Morning,* "and an elegance to the language he used."

Kuralt's sensibility was rooted in his boyhood in Charlotte, where his father headed the city's welfare department and his mother was a social worker. Though the rumpled Kuralt seemed an unlikely candidate for TV, he became CBS's youngest correspondent in 1959. His early assignments took him overseas, including four trips to war-torn Vietnam, but he later admitted, "I wasn't suited to deadline pressure." In 1967, Kuralt began his "On the Road" segments. CBS eminence Walter Cronkite originally regarded them as frivolous but was soon converted, and over the next 13 years, Kuralt would wear out six campers and win 12 Emmys.

Michael Hutchence

With a nuptials pending, the sybaritic singer of INXS apparently takes his own life

To fans left to ponder the latest in a long, sad series of rock-star deaths, INXS's Michael Hutchence, 37, seemed an improbable suicide. Unlike Nirvana's Kurt Cobain, who took his own life in 1994, the Australian native was known not for rage-fueled lyrics but for bringing what London critic Matt Snow called "a cheerful sexiness to rock and roll." Not only had

Hutchence told pals he was looking forward to his band's upcoming 20th-anniversary tour Down Under, but after a string of high-profile flings, he seemed finally to be truly in love. He and flamboyant British TV personality Paula Yates, 37 (who split with rock do-gooder Bob Geldof to take up with Hutchence in 1995), reportedly planned to marry in January on Bora Bora, presumably with their 16-month-old daughter by their side. Instead, on November 21, Hutchence, once known as the "wild man of rock" for his public brawls and open drug use, was found in his hotel suite in Sydney, hanging by a leather belt (and with alcohol and drugs in his system). "He's got a young kid and he sounded so happy," says friend and music writer Ed St. John. "Everyone's just totally baffled."

Allen Ginsberg

Beat also meant beatific
for this poet provocateur

Though his epic *Howl* was loud and
shrill enough to incite an obscenity trial in 1957, when poet Allen Ginsberg,
70, learned that he had fatal liver cancer, he took the news with quiet grace.
A Buddhist for more than two decades,
the tender renegade who, along with

William S. Burroughs

A word addict, the Beat tragedian lusted after drugs,
sexual adventure and the thrill of far-flung places

He was a literary outlaw to some, an apostle of drugs and obscenity to
others. Even his mother called his most famous work, *Naked Lunch,* "that
wretched book." With his Beat Generation pals, William Burroughs, who
died of a heart attack at 83, upended literary conventions as he wrote
about a chaotic, hallucinatory life of often nightmarish involvements with
narcotics, guns and sexual indulgence. Paradoxically, Burroughs was
described by friends as courteous, diffident and dryly humorous. Born in
St. Louis to an office-equipment fortune that evaporated in the 1929
crash, Burroughs graduated from Harvard with only a small stipend to
finance his chosen life of wanderlust. Along an exotic route that ranged
from Dubrovnik and Tangier to Greenwich Village, he became addicted to
morphine and accidentally shot and killed his second wife during a drunken
game in Mexico. That tragedy turned his countenance dark. "I have had no
choice," Burroughs once explained, "but to write my way out."

pals William Burroughs and Jack Kerouac, fueled the Beat movement and inspired a generation of writers and musicians, promptly began phoning his legion of friends to say goodbye. Telling poet Amiri Baraka that he had provided for his lover of 43 years, Peter Orlovsky, Ginsberg added gently, "Do you need any money?"

Such kindness was characteristic of Ginsberg, who grew up in New Jersey in the shadow of his mother Naomi's madness. Afflicted with paranoid psychosis, Naomi, a Russian-born Marxist, died in a mental institution in 1956. Ginsberg's own path was that of a spiritual explorer. He visited ashrams in India and studied Buddhism in Asia but never missed an opportunity to provoke: In 1965 he was deported from Cuba after declaring Ché Guevara to be "cute."

Ironically, the man who made his mark as an agent provocateur left the world as an éminence grise. The author of dozens of volumes of poetry, he was a distinguished professor of English at Brooklyn College. A finalist for the Pulitzer Prize in 1995 and a member of the American Academy of Arts and Letters, Ginsberg collaborated with a range of the leading artists of his time, including Paul McCartney and Philip Glass. His gleeful spirit had charmed public figures from Bob Dylan to Czech President Vaclav Havel. Prolific to the end, Ginsberg composed a dozen poems after learning he had cancer. In the very last, "Death and Fame," he wrote, "I don't care what happens to my body/ Throw ashes in the air." Seven days after receiving his diagnosis, Ginsberg died.

Tony Williams

A rhythm prodigy, he helped liberate Miles and found fusion

When Tony Williams died of a heart attack at 51, the jazz world lost an innovative drummer who didn't so much keep time as conjure with it. Williams had a fluid sense of rhythm. His phrases swirled and surged, tumbling forth in a startling range of volume and color. Encouraged by his father, saxophonist Tillmon Williams, to take up the drums at age 8, Williams was a jazz regular in the Boston area by age of 15. At 17, he was recruited by mercurial trumpet genius Miles Davis to join what would become one of the great bands of the '60s, with Herbie Hancock on piano, Wayne Shorter on saxophone and Ron Carter on bass. The drummer's inventive textures and instinctive reactions cradled and balanced the leader on his restless excursions. By the end of the decade, influenced by Jimi Hendrix, Williams had put more muscle in his sound and launched the first major jazz-rock fusion band, Lifetime, with guitarist John McLaughlin. Pursuing his ideal of music as "the spirit that touches people," Williams in the '80s and '90s studied classical composition, wrote an award-winning piece for strings, piano and percussion, and led traditional bands featuring a new generation of stars.

Sir Georg Solti

He conducted and recorded with unabashed dynamism

His ego was as famously energetic as his baton. Sir Georg Solti, the Hungarian-born conductor who re-established the Chicago Symphony Orchestra as one of the world's great musical instruments, felt competitive not only with classical peers like Herbert Van Karajan and Leonard Bernstein but also with pop stars. "I'm a very vain man," he once admitted, "and I'm very worried about this Mr. Michael Jackson!" More showy than most conductors, with his brash, slashing gestures, he commanded the world stage. During his 22 years as the Chicago orchestra's musical director, he won 30 Grammy Awards, more than any other musician, classical or pop. Knighted in Britain, Sir Georg was also awarded Germany's Knight Commander's Cross.

Unlike many of his contemporaries, Solti never stopped building his repertoire. With the Chicago, he recorded everything from the Romantic symphonies of Beethoven to the contemporary works of Ellen Taaffe Zwilich. Particularly notable was his discovery of the symphonies of Dmitri Shostakovich, including *Symphony No. 13*, a protest against anti-Semitism. Solti's family had perished in the Holocaust, and his own survival was serendipitous: A week before Germany launched World War II, his mother cabled him in Switzerland, where he was visiting Arturo Toscanini, with word not to return to Hungary. Solti settled in Switzerland and, during the war years, made his living playing and teaching the piano. That meant performing with artists who had flourished in Nazi Germany. Solti later conceded he would have done anything to continue making his music. Among his landmark interpretations was his

Pamela Harriman

A hostess par excellence, she
charmed her way up life's ladder

In an earlier age she might have been called a
courtesan, acquiring lovers from St. Moritz to
Palm Springs and amassing money and power in
the process. When Pamela Harriman, the first
female U.S. ambassador to France, died at 76 of
a stroke, she left behind an almost mythic legacy
of politics and passion, notable husbands and
paramours. Daughter of the 11th Baron Digby,
Harriman was taught that a woman's duty was to
please her husband. Her first marriage, at 19, to
Winston Churchill's dissolute son Randolph proved
a disaster, except for the birth of her only child.
But Harriman soon took up with the luminous likes
of newsman Edward R. Murrow and millionaire
diplomat (and onetime New York Governor) Averell
Harriman. After divorcing Churchill she married
Broadway producer Leland Hayward, then six
months after his death wed Harriman. Left with
some $75 million after he died in 1986, she began
wielding clout in her own right as a Democratic
Party fund-raiser. In Paris she used her poise and
vivacity to weave a fabric of friendships for U.S.
interests that, says former Assistant Secretary of
State Richard Holbrooke, "made her the best
ambassador to France we've had in 30 years."

Paul Tsongas

The presidential contender won
hearts in his battle with cancer

Though beloved for his basic decency and
respected for his brave fight against illness,
Democrat Paul Tsongas will be best remembered
for his keen sense of responsibility. Struck by
cancer in 1983, the U.S. Senator from Massachusetts walked away from his dream job to be
with his wife and three daughters. Eight years
later, his lymphoma in remission and a bone-
marrow transplant behind him, he launched a
long-shot presidential bid, stressing that his
campaign issues of fiscal responsibility and
personal sacrifice were inspired by feelings of
family obligation. "I want to do the things [that
will make] my grandchildren feel good about me,"
he said. Tsongas died at 55 of pneumonia.

Deng Xiaoping

He freed China's economy, but then came Tiananmen

"Leaders are men, not gods," he once said. Yet Deng Xiaoping, an avid fan of soccer and bridge, was capable of ruthless tyranny untempered by humanity. The darkest moment of his 11-year reign as China's "paramount leader" came in 1989 when he ordered a military crackdown on pro-democracy forces at Tiananmen Square. That assault and China's subsequent backslide into isolation irreparably sullied his reputation. When he died at 92 from respiratory complications, Deng left a mixed legacy of enlightened economic programs and benighted political terror.

A child of the rural countryside, Deng left home at age 16 and won a scholarship to France, where he first sampled communist theory. By 1926 he was in Moscow, studying Marxist-Leninist doctrine. Dispatched to Guangxi province to spread the faith, he met Mao Zedong, whose bold guerrilla strategy appealed to Deng. Their youthful alliance gave rise to China's infamous Red Army and would prove steadfast until the Great Leap Forward. The mass starvation attending that wayward modernization campaign convinced Deng to embrace a more pragmatic economic strategy summarized in his famous maxim: "It doesn't matter if the cat is black or white, as long as it catches mice." For such liberal thinking he was purged as a "capitalist roader" during the Cultural Revolution of the mid-1960s, then exalted as a visionary during the less dogmatic 1980s. (In 1988 he posed, forefront above, in a photo flashback to Mao's famed earlier swim.)

Through it all, including Deng's last three years blighted by Parkinson's disease, Zhuo Lin, the third of his wives and mother of their five children, stayed by his side. At the very end, tens of thousands of Chinese lined Beijing's Avenue of Eternal Peace to catch a final glimpse as a 35-car motorcade escorted Deng's body to a crematory. "Xiaoping was a good comrade," said one onlooker. "Most of us here would be poor if it were not for him."

The Notorious B.I.G.

A crack dealer turned rapper, he created an art about death and got gunned down at 24

Christopher Wallace—aka the Notorious B.I.G. and Biggie Smalls—was convinced that his second hip-hop album, *Life After Death . . . 'Til Death Do Us Part,* would secure his place at the top of the rap pack. The former crack dealer felt that one cut in particular—"You're Nobody ('Til Somebody Kills You)"—was destined for the charts. Eerily, two weeks before the album's release, Wallace, 24, was fatally shot in a fusillade of fire while driving home from L.A.'s Soul Train Awards. The roadway killing was a chilling replay of the shooting of Tupac Shakur, a rival rapper who had once been Wallace's friend. Because Wallace and Shakur were the central figures in a much-publicized feud between rap's East and West Coast factions, there was speculation—but no proof—that the Wallace murder was retaliation for Shakur's. At 6'3" and upward of 300 lbs., Wallace cut a menacing figure on the Brooklyn streets where he grew up the son of a single mom who taught preschool. He himself left behind his estranged wife, rapper Faith Evans, 24, their 5-month-old son and a 3-year-old girl by an earlier relationship. (In his own last record, Shakur made a veiled, taunting reference to sleeping with Evans.) Busted on drug charges at 17, Wallace spent nine months in jail, then sought hope in music and debuted with *Ready to Die,* a song cycle about a dealer driven to suicide. "I thought Tupac's death was a wake-up call," said fellow rapper Ahmir in mourning. "I guess we hit the snooze button."

Laura Nyro

Her stoned soul picnic of sound has nourished every female singer since

Her distinctive, octave-ranging wail may not have had chart-topping appeal, but the sensuous, intensely personal music she wrote—with its elastic tempos, introspective lyrics and quirky mix of folk, soul and rock—demonstrably did. During her 49 years, singer/songwriter Laura Nyro penned many songs that others turned into hits, including "Wedding Bell Blues" and "Stoned Soul Picnic" (The Fifth Dimension), "Eli's Coming" (Three Dog Night), "And When I Die" (Blood, Sweat and Tears) and "Stoney End" (Barbra Streisand). In her life, as in her music, the Bronx-born pianist marched to her own beat. In junior high Nyro ducked out at night to sing in subway stations with a Puerto Rican a cappella group. She cut high school classes shamelessly ("I just couldn't get educated in school"), never learned to read music and adopted purple nail polish and black clothes long before they were chic. She also wrote pop's first lesbian love song ("Emmie," released in 1968). At her death from ovarian cancer, Nyro was survived by her son from a three-year marriage and by her longtime female companion.

Fela

The Nigerian saxophonist was both a pop star and a prisoner of conscience

Africa's most famous musician, Fela spiked his roiling rhythms with pointed lyrics denouncing the leaders of his authoritarian country. "Nigeria is worse than South Africa," he once said. "In Nigeria, blacks mistreat blacks." For his efforts he was jailed at least a dozen times. The son of an Anglican priest and a female nationalist, Fela Anikulapo-Kuti was influenced by American jazz, which he encountered while studying classical music in London. Concocting his own unique fusion of funk, jazz and traditional African rhythms, he also developed a distinct stage presence, often performing in only bikini underwear. In 1978 he married 27 of his dancing girls in a single ceremony, all but eight of whom left him while he was jailed. After suffering from AIDS, Fela died of a heart attack at 58.

Jacques Cousteau

He made his life an odyssey—
and invited the world to swim along

To Jacques-Yves Cousteau being underwater was the closest place to heaven on earth. "When you dive," he said, "you begin to feel that you're an angel." By the time Cousteau died at 87 of a respiratory infection and heart problems, the environmentalist had spent more than half a century probing and drama-tizing the secrets of the sea. His achievements—among them the 1956 Oscar-winning documentary *The Silent World*, his TV series, *The Undersea World of Jacques Cousteau*, which gained 40 Emmy nominations, and his codevelopment of the Aqua-Lung—made him the most famous and beloved Frenchman on the globe. Known in France as *le Commandant*, Cousteau in 1980 was urged to run for President. "His life," says French President Jacques Chirac, "resembles an adventure."

The adventure was not without sadness—and a hint of *scandale*. Cousteau was devastated by the 1979 death, in a seaplane accident, of his younger

William Brennan

A forceful thinker and a wily negotiator, he put his stamp on the Supreme Court

The U.S. Constitution had an extraordinary advocate in Supreme Court Justice William J. Brennan Jr. During his 34 years on the high court—a tenure surpassed by only five predecessors—Brennan earned a reputation as a genial yet unyielding warrior for the founding document and the individual rights it sought to protect. "To strike another blow for freedom allows a man to walk a little taller and raise his head a little higher," he wrote. "And while he can, he must." Brennan's compassion for the downtrodden came from growing up as the second of eight children born to Irish immigrants in Newark, New Jersey. His father, a laborer at a brewery, rose to become a union leader. When Brennan died at 91 he left a legacy of judicial activism that qualified him as one of the most influential—and beguiling—justices in U.S. history. As Justice Antonin Scalia, a staunch conservative, put it, "Even those who disagree with him the most love him."

son Philippe and later feuded with elder son Jean-Michel over commercial use of the family name. Following the 1990 death of his first wife, the filmmaker wed a former flight attendant who, by then, had given birth to two children by Cousteau. He once admitted, "I regret not having given enough time to my children." What he gave the rest of the world, though, were front-row seats to the mysteries of the deep. "Scientists tend to talk in terms of science, and no one else understands what they're saying," says British environmentalist Cecilia Weckstrom. "But Cousteau used concepts that really touched the man on the street."

James Dickey

A writer of muscular verse found fame with *Deliverance*

He drank hard. He flirted outrageously. And when he put pen to paper his subjects were unreconstructedly masculine: fighter pilots, football players and, most famously, good old boys in a canoe. But years before James Dickey burst into popular view with his 1970 novel *Deliverance* (followed two years later by the movie he both wrote and appeared in as a portly sheriff), he was already making his way as a poet, eventually publishing some 20 volumes.

Born in Atlanta, Dickey played varsity football at Clemson and flew more than 100 missions in World War II. His first marriage lasted 28 years, and the gossip mills whirled when he wed one of his students at the University of South Carolina just two months after his wife's death. But for all his swagger, Dickey, father of three, seemed to be a firm family man. "God, I love my children!" he burst out to a friend shortly before he died from lung disease at 73.

Harold Robbins

His list of credits included 20 novels, five wives and a big ego

Though critics begged to differ, author Harold Robbins, who died from pulmonary arrest at 81, claimed that he would be remembered as "the best writer in the world." He parlayed a predictable mix of racy sex, money and power tussles into potboilers that sold more than 50 million copies in 40 countries. *The Carpetbaggers* and *The Betsy* became movies, enabling a dropout who grew up in foster homes to support a lifestyle that included several lavish residences, a yacht and a gambling habit worthy of one of his heroes.

James A. Michener

Embracing life, he wrote sprawling, old-fashioned novels the old-fashioned way

James A. Michener approached death like the word warrior he was. For years the author of historical sagas (*Hawaii, The Source, Texas*) had continued to write despite hip surgery, a bypass operation and debilitating thrice-weekly dialysis sessions at a treatment center near his modest home in Austin, Texas. Admittedly, Michener found his resolve flagging after Mari, his wife of 39 years, died of cancer in 1994. "Then I said, 'Wait a minute. This is very dangerous thinking,' " he recalled, " 'and we are not going down that road.' " But early in October he asked to be taken off dialy-

sis and, by all accounts, slipped away peacefully at 90.

The son of a Pennsylvania widow who supported herself by taking in laundry and raising orphaned children, Michener escaped his hardscrabble childhood by winning a scholarship to Swarthmore College. Though he chased adventure, surviving a bull in Pamplona and three plane crashes, he was otherwise an austere Quaker with few pleasures aside from opera. A self-described "fiery liberal," he made one failed run for Congress and donated $117 million to charity. Michener's astonishing literary success made it possible. His first book, *Tales of the South Pacific,* which didn't appear until he was 40, won the 1948 Pulitzer Prize and was the basis for the smash musical. Over the next half century, Michener sold more than 75 million copies of some 40 books. Though critics tended to dismiss his epics, Michener claimed only to create the sort of novels he liked to read. "I have never called myself an author," he declared in his memoir. "I am a writer."

Ben Hogan

Before Arnie, Jack or Tiger, there was 'The Hawk'

Famously private and taciturn, Ben Hogan offered four words of advice when Nick Faldo, himself a Masters champion, flew to Texas a few years back to ask the great one how to win the U.S. Open: "Shoot the lowest score." By heeding his own sardonic counsel, Hogan won 64 golf tournaments—including nine majors—securing his place as one of the sport's all-time greats.

And perhaps its most courageous. At mid-career in 1949, Hogan was nearly killed when a bus crashed head-on into his car on a two-lane Texas highway late at night. At impact, he dove to his right to shield his wife, Valerie (with him, left, in 1948), lessening her injuries but increasing his own. Doctors told him he would be lucky to walk again. But in one of the most stirring comebacks ever he won the 1950 U.S. Open. Despite being limited by his condition to only about half a dozen tourneys a year, Hogan went on to win the British Open, two Masters titles and three of his four U.S. Opens. "He asked no quarter and he gave none," says Byron Nelson, 85, another links legend. Hogan continued to daunt the competition after retiring from the PGA tour in 1971. For years, golfers at Hogan's beloved Shady Oaks Country Club in Fort Worth routinely waffled on the 9th and 18th holes. According to club lore, it wasn't the difficult terrain but the knowledge that Hogan, dubbed "The Hawk," was watching from his favorite clubhouse table.

He was not to the country club born. His father, a Texas blacksmith, committed suicide when Ben was 9, and the boy learned to play while caddying for 65 cents a round. When Hogan died at 84, after Alzheimer's disease and cancer, Jack Nicklaus said, "Golf has lost the best shotmaker the game has ever seen."

Curt Flood

His legal war helped free and enrich ballplayers

Baseball fans still talk about Curt Flood's impressive record during his 12 seasons with the St. Louis Cardinals—he was a .293 lifetime hitter and an All-Star center fielder who won the Gold Glove fielding title seven years in a row. Yet when he died at 59 from throat cancer and related pneumonia, his colleagues remembered—and thanked—Flood for his bravura performance on a different field of dreams: the courtroom. With his legal challenge of baseball's "reserve clause," he eventually freed players from contractual bondage to a specific team. Flood launched his attack in 1969 after the Cards tried to trade him to the Philadelphia Phillies. Determined not to be relocated without his consent, Flood sued to be sprung from the controversial clause. When he was asked in court which team he wanted to play for, he answered, "The team that makes me the best offer." After Flood's court petition failed, he played just two months with the Washington Senators, then quit baseball for good. But his initiative emboldened other players to take up a fight that would culminate in 1976 with the dawning of the age of free agency and seven-figure salaries.

Harry Helmsley

A self-made, staid king of means got famous marrying the queen of mean

Billionaire Harry Helmsley began work as a $12-a-week office boy in New York City in 1925 and bought his first building for $1,000 during the depths of the Depression. He lived the life of a sedate—if successful—businessman until he divorced his first wife in 1971 after 33 years of marriage. Then Harry wed Leona Roberts—and his world got a dramatic makeover. Together, Harry and Leona, a flamboyant former model who had become a top-earning broker at one of Harry's sales offices, entertained lavishly at their 28-room Connecticut mansion and Manhattan penthouse complete with swimming pool.

The public ostentation ended abruptly in 1988 when the pair was indicted for tax evasion. While Harry was found mentally unfit to stand trial, the autocratic Leona was convicted in 1989 and packed off to federal prison for 18 months. After her release the couple lived in seclusion. When Harry died at 87 from pneumonia, Leona said, "My fairy tale is over," then ordered the floodlights dimmed on the Empire State Building, the crown jewel of their partnership holdings, which included 50,000 apartments and 27 hotels across the U.S.

Rosie the Riveter

Rose Monroe embodied the can-do spirit of America's war-era women

In 1944, while on location at a Michigan aircraft factory shooting a film plugging war bonds, actor Walter Pidgeon stumbled on Rose  **Monroe. A real, live Rosie the Riveter—the fictitious working woman long celebrated on posters and in song—Monroe had a job pounding rivets into B-24 and B-29 bombers. Pidgeon signed her for the film, and the rest is history. Though most U.S. women quit their jobs after VJ Day, Monroe, who died at 77 of kidney failure, embodied Rosie's self-reliance to the end. Never trading on her fleeting celebrity, she founded a construction firm specializing in luxury homes.**

We Can Do It!

Roberto Goizueta

A Cuban émigré jumbled the Coke formula but wound up pleasing both Main and Wall Street

It's not quite the classic rags to riches tale. After all, Roberto Goizueta was born to wealth in Batista's Cuba, was shipped abroad for a Yale education, then landed a slot as a chemist at the Havana offices of Coca Cola. But when it came time in 1961 for Goizueta and his wife to flee Castro's Cuba, the couple left with only a suitcase, 100 shares of Coke stock—and, of course, his door-opening degree. Taking a job with the soft-drink colossus in Florida, he rose swiftly, heading Coke's labs by 1974—a position that made him one of only two chemists allowed to memorize the cola's lucrative secret formula.

Seven years later, he was tapped to run the company—and a legend was born. By the time of his death at 65 from lung cancer, Goizueta had emerged as one of his adopted country's preeminent CEOs, credited with championing the strategy of boosting shareholder value. During his 16-year watch, Coke dominated the $54 billion carbonated-beverage business, and its Wall Street worth increased an astounding 3,500 percent from $4 billion to $150 billion. Seemingly blessed with a Midas touch, Goizueta turned even his worst mistakes into bottom-line bonanzas: The disastrous launch of New Coke provoked a surge in the sale of "classic" Coke, and his misguided purchase of Columbia Pictures later proved profitable when he sold the film studio to Sony. "No one loved the Coca-Cola company more than Roberto," said board member Warren Buffett. "He was a great leader and a great gentleman."

Burgess Meredith

Skilled at Shakespeare, he found fame as *Rocky's* trainer and *Batman's* penguin

In the 65 years after he made his Broadway debut as a duck in a New York City production of *Alice in Wonderland*, Burgess Meredith became one of the great Shakespearean actors of his time. Yet when he died at 89 of pneumonia and complications from Alzheimer's disease, Meredith was best known for his comedic turns, first as the villainous Penguin in the mid-1960s' *Batman* TV series, then as Sylvester Stallone's raspy-voiced trainer in four Rocky pictures. "Burgess," says *Batman* star Adam West, "had a great sense of the absurd."

Perhaps it was that sensibility that enabled Meredith

to survive an Ohio childhood that he characterized as "grim and incoherent." His doctor father was alcoholic and abusive toward his mother, who left Meredith's rearing largely to his older sister. A boy soprano, he moved to New York City at 10 to attend a cathedral choir school. He made it to Amherst College, then dropped out to pursue acting. Four times married, three times divorced, Meredith had affairs with many of the leading ladies of his day: Ingrid Bergman, Marlene Dietrich, Hedy Lamarr and Tallulah Bankhead (whom he first met, he recalled, when she answered the door at her Manhattan apartment naked). Briefly blacklisted during the 1950s, he worked steadily after he was cast in 1954's *Advise and Consent*. By the time he shot 1993's *Grumpy Old Men*, Meredith was battling Alzheimer's and had to rely on cue cards. Director Donald Petrie, who was unaware of Meredith's condition, recalls thinking, "I hope I'm doing that good at his age."

David Doyle

Surmounting personal loss, he found heaven among *Angels*

Although theater was his first love, Broadway-trained actor David Doyle never quibbled with the TV gig that fed him. "*Charlie's Angels* ain't *Hamlet*," he said about the ABC jigglethon that made him famous, "but it sure is entertaining." From 1976 to 1981, Doyle, who died of a heart attack at 67, played the avuncular go-between for the gal gumshoes and their unseen titular boss. "He was so quick to laugh and to smile," recalls Kate Jackson (right).

That joie de vivre was hard won. Doyle's first wife died from an accidental staircase fall, leaving Doyle to care for their young daughter. His second wife was diagnosed with a disease that left her nearly blind. Yet even in tough times, Doyle—known to a new generation as the voice of Grandpa on Nickelodeon's *Rugrats*—maintained his good humor. "This," he said of himself, "is one happy man."

Brian Keith

Cancer and a daughter's suicide proved an overwhelming burden

He played everything from a homicidal rancher to a stone-faced private detective. But gruff, burly ex-Marine Brian Keith was best known for his roles as a family man. He starred onscreen in 1961's *The Parent Trap*, and was the kindly Uncle Bill, who from 1966 to 1971 raised orphaned twins and a teenager on TV's *Family Affair*. Sadly, Keith's trademark confidence apparently faltered in the face of his advanced lung cancer and despair over the suicide of his actress daughter, Daisy, 27. Two and a half months after her death, family members found Keith, 75, dead. Like Daisy, he had died of a self-inflicted gunshot wound. *Family Affair* twin Johnny Whitaker said that Keith, who always made sure the set was a positive place for his young costars, "was a real Uncle Bill."

Jeane Dixon

To some she was a syndicated seer; others saw bull rising

Her astrological muse was not always reliable. She predicted, for instance, that World War III would erupt in 1958 and that the Soviets would land the first person on the moon. But after John F. Kennedy was assassinated in 1963, Jeane Dixon became America's hottest psychic. Seven years earlier, in an interview with *Parade* magazine, Dixon had forecast that a tall Democrat with thick brown hair and blue eyes would be elected President in 1960, then would die in office. After the Dallas shooting, Dixon, a Roman Catholic, said she had based her prophecy on a vision that came to her in 1952 while she was at prayer; she also maintained that she had foreseen an assassination but that *Parade* had refused to print that.

Right up to her death at 79 of a heart attack, Dixon, who was known as the Seeress of Washington, inspired both ardent admiration and sneering skepticism. Fans cited the oft-quoted story of how, when Dixon was 8, a gypsy soothsayer foretold the girl's gift for prophecy. Detractors of her popular syndicated column gloated at her goofs, including her 1992 forecast of a loss for Bill Clinton. Though Bush took a lickin', Dixon kept right on predictin'.

Harry Blackstone

His classic brand of magic startled, amused and dazzled audiences

Harry Blackstone Jr. was just 6 months old and in diapers when he made his debut in one of his dad's disappearing illusions. After Harry Sr. died in 1965, Harry Jr. took over the franchise and turned it into a lively comedy of dancing handkerchiefs, sawed-up bodies (usually his wife's) and floating lightbulbs. Twice named Magician of the Year, Blackstone, who died at 62 of pancreatic cancer, enjoyed a three-decade run on the magic circuit.

Jeanne Calment

She enjoyed her days—and got more of them than anyone

In 1875, the year Jeanne Louise Calment was born in Arles, in southern France, Victoria was Queen and no one had yet invented the telephone, the electric light or the flush toilet. By the time Calment died In August at 122, she had lived the longest life ever documented, according to *The Guinness Book of World Records,* far outlasting her husband, her only child and her only grandchild. Asked how she had managed to endure so long, she once joked, "I think God must have forgotten me." But she was never overlooked by the residents of Arles, who would turn out each year for a birthday party. "She was the living memory of our city," a local politician said. In fact, she could recall in 1888 meeting neighbor Vincent Van Gogh, whom she called "ugly, disagreeable, sick." Calment gave up smoking in 1995, not for health reasons but because she could no longer see well enough to light a cigarette. She believed in the daily benefit of port wine, olive oil and humor. When someone would depart, saying, "Until next year, perhaps," she would reply: "I don't see why not. You don't look so bad to me."

PICTURE CREDITS

COVER Diana: UK Press • Brad Pitt: Alex Oliveira/Rex USA • Heather Locklear: Larry Levine/Globe Photos • Will Smith: Michael O'Neill/Outline • Chelsea Clinton: Richard Ellis/Sygma • George Clooney: Michael O'Neill/Outline • Ellen DeGeneres: Andrew Eccles/Outline • **Title Page** Red Skelton: Archive Photos • **Table of Contents** Hanson: Danny Clinch/Outline • Gianni Versace and Courtney Love: Gerardo Somoza/Outline • **Back Cover** Spice Girls: Stephen Ellison/Outline (top); Harrison Ford: Timothy White/Outline

GOODBYE, DIANA 4 John Giles/PA • 5 Russell Boyce/Reuters/Archive Photos • 6 (clockwise, from top) Big Pictures/FSP; Big Pictures; AP/Wide World Photos • 7 Gregory Pace/Sygma • 8 UK Press (top); John Gaps III/AP/Wide World Photos • 9 John Zich/IPOL, Inc. • 10 (clockwise, from top left) Alpha/Globe Photos; Adam Butler/PA; David Jones/PA • 11 Patrick DeMarchelier/Camera Press/Globe Photos • 12 (clockwise, from top left) Chris Bacon/PA; Robert Wallis/SABA; Francois Mori/AP/Wide World Photos; AP Photo/Pool • 13 Mike Hutchings/Reuters/Archive Photos (top); Ken Goff

HEADLINERS 14 R. Simons/Sygma • 15 Patrick Davison/Rocky Mountain News/Sygma • 16 George Kalinsky • 17 Reuters/Mike Segar/Archive Photos (top); Reuters/Peter Morgan/Archive Photos • 18 C.J. Gunther/Pool/Sipa • 19 (clockwise, from top left) Matt Stone/AP/Wide World Photos; Steven Senne/AP/Wide World Photos; Peter Byrne/Guzelian (2) • 20 Jim Bourg/Reuters/Archive Photos • 21 Arturo Mari/AP/Wide World Photos (top); Outline • 22 Taro Yamasaki (top); Robert Petry/Gamma Liaison • 23 Charles Bennett/AP/Wide World Photos (top); U.S. Army/Reuters/Archive Photos • 24 (clockwise, from top right) Dirck Halstead/Gamma Liaison; Puskar/AP/Wide World Photos; Christopher Little/Outline • 25 Lawrence Schwartzwald/Gamma Liaison • 26 Courtesy Dorothy Hutelmyer (top); Michael A. Schwarz • 27 Keystone • 28 Reuters/Jim Bourg/Archive Photos (top); Jonathan Exley/Gamma Liaison • 29 Jeffrey Lowe (top); Mark J. Terrill/AP/Wide World Photos • 30 Sharon Farmer/The White House • 31 (clockwise, from top right) J. Scott Applewhite/ AP/Wide World Photos; John Todd/AP/Wide World Photos; Robert Giroux/Reuters/Archive Photos • 32 Kermani/Gamma Liaison • 33 Taro Yamasaki (left); DPA/Mark Davitt/Gamma Liaison (7) • 34 Peter Morgan/Reuters/Archive Photos • 35 David Karp/AP/Wide World Photos (top); Rick Maiman/Sygma • 36 Scott Teitler/Retna Ltd., USA • 37 (from top) Patrick McMullan/ Gamma Liaison; Gerardo Somoza/Outline; Savino/Sipa • 38-39 (clockwise, from top left) Stephen Ellison/Outline; Stephen Crowley/The New York Times; Mike Nelson/ Reuters/ Archive Photos; Mike Nelson/Reuters/Archive Photos • 40 Ron Edmonds/AP/Wide World Photos • 41 (clockwise, from top right) Jack Smith/AP/Wide World Photos; Rupert Thorpe/ Online USA Inc.; James Kelly/Globe Photos; Ron Sachs/Consolidated News Photos/Archive Photos • 42 AP/Wide World Photos/Ramapo High School Yearbook • 43 AP/Wide World Photos/WNBC-TV (top); Daniel Hulshizer/AP/Wide World Photos • 44 Chip Simons • 45 Ann Summa (top); Axel Koester/Sygma • 46 Anne Fishbein/Sygma • 47 (from top) Reuters/ CBS Evening News/Archive Photos; Alan Tannenbaum/Sygma; AP/Wide World Photos/HO • 48 (from top) Reuters/Mike Segar/Archive Photos; Schonburg Center/Van Hasselt/Sygma; Kathy Willens/AP/Wide World Photos • 49 Edward Barrington/Sygma • 50 Photri (top); AP/Wide World Photos • 51 Murdo MacLeod (top); Ken Goff • 52 Dave Martin/AP/Wide World Photos • 53 Albert Ferreira/Globe Photos (left); Tom Pidgeon/AP/Wide World Photos • 54 KC/Pool/Adam Butler/Reuters/Archive Photos (top); Joe De Maria/ Sygma • 55 Peter Diana/ Pittsburgh Post Gazette (left); Andy Hayt/NBA Photos

SENSATIONS 56 Andrew Eccles/Outline • 57 Todd France • 58 Michael Watts/Mazur • 59 Kevin Winter/Celebrity Photo • 60 Reuters/Blake Sell/Archive Photos • 61 Christopher Little/Outline (top); Chris Cole/Duomo • 62 Everett Collection (top); Steve Kagan • 63 Jim Smeal/Galella Ltd. (top); David Strick/Outline • 64 Chris Haston/NBC • 65 Walter McBride/Retna Ltd. USA • 66 George Holz/Outline • 67 Outline • 68 John Chiasson/Outline (top); David Allocca/DMI • 69 Guy Aroch/Retna Ltd. USA • 70 Aaron Rapoport/ Outline • 71 Reuters/Barbara L. Johnston/Archive Photos; © Marc Brown 1997 • 72 Ian Cook • 73 Susan Shacter/Outline • 74 APL/Peter Brennan/Retna Ltd. USA • 75 (clockwise, from top left) Gamma Liaison; Gillian Helfgott; Michael Le Poer Trench • 76 Dana Fineman/Sygma • 77 Armando Gallo/Retna Ltd. USA

STYLE 78-79 Martin Schoeller/SABA • 79 (from top) Patrick McMullan/UPM/London Features; Tim Mosenfelder/Corbis; David Allen/Corbis • 80 (clockwise, from top right) Miranda Shen/Celebrity Photos; Janet Gough/Celebrity Photo; Ken Babolcsay/London Features Int'l; Gregg DeGuire/London Features Int'l; Nick Elgar/London Features Int'l; Ron Wolfson/Online USA Inc.; Gilbert Flores/Celebrity Photo • 81 (from top) Kimberly Butler; Norman Y. Lono/NYT Pictures; Kimberly Butler • 82-83 Dan Borris/Outline • 83 Greg Gorman/Gamma Liaison (top); Patrick Swirc/MPA/Gamma Liaison • 84 (clockwise, from top right) Steve Granitz/Retna Ltd. USA; Timothy White/Outline; Tammie Arroyo/South Beach Photo; Roger Karnbad/Celebrity • 85 (clockwise, from top right) Kevin Mazur; Lisa Rose/Globe Photos; John Spellman/Retna Ltd. USA; Pat/Arnal/Stills/Retna Ltd. USA

FAMILY MATTERS 86-87 Lenhof-Rat/Gamma Liaison • 88 F. Trapper/Sygma (left); Andrea Renault/Globe Photos • 89 (clockwise, from top left) James Schnepf/Gamma Liaison; Janet Gough/Celebrity Photo; Santiago Baez/Sipa; Santiago Baez/Sipa • 90 (clockwise, from top left) Gary Moss; Fred Prouser/Sipa; Phil Roach/IPOL Inc. • 91 (clockwise, from top left) Scott Downie/Celebrity Photo; Fred Prouser/Sipa; Barry King/Gamma Liaison • 92 (clockwise, from top left) George Lange/Outline; Terry O'Neill/Sygma; Michele McDonald/Gamma Liaison • 93 (clockwise, from top left) Beth Gwinn/Retna Ltd. USA; Lisa Rose/Globe Photos; Steve Granitz/Retna Ltd. USA • 94 Kaish-Dahl • 95 Walter P. Calahan • 96 Jay Spence (top); Olympia/Gamma Liaison • 97 (clockwise, from top right) © Lisa Smith/Photolink; Michael Springer/Gamma Liaison; Christopher Little/Outline • 98 (clockwise, from top left) Richard Ellis/Sygma; James Bevins/Big Pictures USA; Pentimento Entertainment • 99 (clockwise, from top left) Kevin Winter/Celebrity Photo; Lisa O'Connor/Celebrity Photo; Wattie Cheung/CP/Retna Ltd. USA • 100 AP/Wide World Photos (top); Allan Zasi • 101 Photograph by JK Isaac copyright ©1997 Triumph International Inc. published under license owned by OK! Magazine • 102 (clockwise, from top left) Jim Smeal/Galella Ltd.; Jim Smeal/Galella Ltd.; Jim Smeal /Galella Ltd.; Eddie Sanderson/Shooting Star • 103 (clockwise, from top left) Chris Casaburi/Gamma Liaison; James Bevins/Galella Ltd.; Greg Gorman/Gamma Liaison; Janet Gough/Celebrity Photo • 104 John Zich • 105 Jim McHugh/Outline • 106 Michael Carroll • 106-107 (insets) Courtesy of the Featherstones • 107 Acey Harper (2)

TRIBUTE 108 Ted Allan/MPTV • 109 Everett Collection (top); Eric Skipsey/MPTV • 110 Jim McHugh/Outline • 111 David Strick/Outline • 112 Globe Photos • 113 Archive Photos • 114 Mike Segar/Sipa • 114-115 Eddie Adams/Outline • 116 Globe Photos • 117 Johnny Rozsa/Outline • 118 Abramson/Sipa • 119 Snowden/Camera Press/Retna Ltd. USA (top); AP/Wide World Photos • 120 Mitchell Levy/Rangefinders/Globe Photos • 121 Laura Levine/Outline • 122 Dan Chavkin/Outline • 122-123 New York Times Co./Archive Photos • 124 David Redfern/Retna Ltd. USA • 125 Terry O'Neill/London Records • 126 Nora Feller/Retna Ltd. USA (top); Reuters/Brian Snyder/Archive Photos •127 XINHUA/Chine Nouvelle/Gamma Liaison • 128 Geoffrey De Boismenu/Outline • 129 Gary Gershoff/Retna Ltd. USA (top); Sipa • 130 AP/Wide World Photos • 131 Archive Photos • 132 Lou Krasky/ AP/Wide World Photos (top); Paul Harris/Outline • 133 Tim Boule/Outline • 134 Loomis Dean/LIFE • 135 UPI/Corbis-Bettmann • 136 (clockwise, from top left) Douglas Kirkland/ Sygma; AP/Wide World Photos/National Archives; AP/Wide World Photos • 137 Michael O'Neill/Outline • 138 Nancy Ellison/Sygma • 139 Steve Schapiro/Sygma (top); Screen Scenes • 140 Dennis Brack/Black Star • 141 UPI/Corbis-Bettmann (top); Jean Pierre Fizet/Sygma